Hong Kong

The return of Hong Kong in 1997 could bring China countless political and economic benefits bolstering both its already rapidly expanding economy and its international standing. The potential gains are undeniable, but there are no guarantees that China will harness the colony's full potential. Crucially, it is China's handling of the transition that will decide whether an opportunity is seized or missed.

This study explores the challenges that Chinese policy makers face up to 1997 and beyond: the clash of political cultures; handling problematic negotiations; and dealing with conflicting economic interests. Michael Yahuda assesses the Chinese motives and agendas that inform both Sino-British negotiations and relations between the communist authorities and the inhabitants of Hong Kong.

This is a valuable contribution to the debate about the future of Hong Kong under Chinese rule which recognises that it is essential for China to adopt a *laissez-faire* approach to the colony and its lucrative markets. Failure to do so will have serious consequences for the future of China itself.

Michael Yahuda is Reader in International Relations at the London School of Economics and Political Science, University of London.

Hong Kong

China's challenge

Michael Yahuda

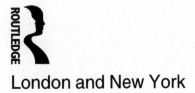

London and New York

First published 1996
by Routledge
11 New Fetter Lane, London EC4P 4EE

Simultaneously published in the USA and Canada
by Routledge
29 West 35th Street, New York, NY 10001

Reprinted 1996

Typeset in Times by Routledge
Printed and bound in Great Britain by
TJ Press (Padstow) Ltd, Padstow, Cornwall

British Library Cataloguing in Publication Data
A catalogue record for this book is available from the British Library

Library of Congress Cataloguing in Publication Data
Yahuda, Michael B.
Hong Kong: China's challenge/Michael Yahuda.
    p. cm. – (Routledge in Asia)
1. Hong Kong – Politics and government. 2. China – Politics and government
– 1976- I. Title. II. Series.
DS796.H757Y34 1996
951.2505–dc20   95–52273
                                                            CIP

ISBN 0–415–14070–6 (hbk)
ISBN 0–415–14071–4 (pbk)

For Tamar, Daniella and David

Contents

Foreword

The constitutional status of Hong Kong was clarified in 1984 through an Anglo-Chinese treaty whereby the government in Beijing would assume sovereignty on 1 July 1997. That treaty also made provision for the political future of the territory which was to become a Special Administrative Region of the People's Republic with a high degree of autonomy. The initial, if guarded, optimism which greeted the Anglo-Chinese accord has given way in the intervening years to a growing apprehension about how the government in Beijing will interpret and apply its terms. The critical precipitating factor in the adverse change in the climate of relations between the government in Beijing with those in both Hong Kong and London was the massacre of pro-democracy demonstrators in Tiananmen Square in June 1989. That bloody episode and the popular reaction within Hong Kong caused the Chinese government to view the territory as a source of subversion and a threat to the established political order in the People's Republic. Attempts by successive Governors of Hong Kong to sustain popular confidence within the territory through promoting the construction of a new airport and to widen the bases of democratic participation were construed in Beijing as political challenges – one response being a public commitment to replace Hong Kong's elected Legislative Council on the morrow of the transfer of sovereignty. The main issue, as that moment of transfer approaches, is whether China will honour its pledge to allow Hong Kong to maintain its rule of law and basic freedoms that have been responsible for its remarkable economic success from which the People's Republic has greatly benefited.

Michael Yahuda takes this question beyond the important issue of the predicament facing Hong Kong and its people to that of whether or not China's political leaders will see the assumption of sovereignty as an opportunity to be grasped to national advantage. He has identified and addressed a dimension of the problematic future of Hong Kong that has been neglected in the literature. The future of Hong Kong, as he puts it, is a critical test for China as it sustains its commitment to economic modernisation, faces the issue of political succession and seeks to effect unification with Taiwan on its own terms. With respect to the latter, how China handles Hong Kong will be the first test of the formula of 'one country two systems' invented with Taiwan in mind. Well beyond that, as Michael Yahuda writes, 'a display of tolerance for an autonomous Hong Kong would consolidate its new relations with the Chinese communities outside China, strengthen Beijing's stance regarding Taiwan, reduce anxieties in Southeast Asia, ease China's relations with the USA, enhance the process of China's integration with the Asia-Pacific region, and improve China's international standing generally'.

The great merit of this succinct and profound analysis of the challenge facing China in assuming sovereignty over Hong Kong is that it has identified a likely turning point in China's role and place within international society. Without disregarding the domestic problems that may be posed for China's leadership in fulfilling the spirit as well as the letter of the Anglo-Chinese accord, it explores a dimension of China's assumption of sovereignty over Hong Kong which has wide-ranging international significance in a post-Cold War world. For that reason, this book not only makes a scholarly contribution to an understanding of China's position and prospects in seeking to assimilate Hong Kong, but also to a central and critical issue in China's foreign policy at the turn of the century.

Michael Leifer

Acknowledgements

In the writing of this book I have benefited greatly from the interviews and discussions with officials, scholars, business people and journalists in Hong Kong, London, Beijing and Washington. Most of these cannot be named for obvious reasons, but it is with pleasure that I acknowledge the help and encouragement of Joseph Cheng, Simon Holberton, Brian Hook, Michael Leifer, Simon Long, Jonathan Mirsky, Gerald Segal, David Shambaugh, Wang Gungwu, Byron Weng and Dick Wilson. Needless to say, none of them (or those I have not mentioned by name) is responsible for any of the shortcomings this book may possess.

Finally, I am most grateful for the following bodies who provided me with financial assisstance: the Nuffield Foundation Small Grants to visit Beijing and Hong Kong in the summer of 1992; the British Academy to visit Beijing twice, in February and July 1995; and the International Studies Fund of my college, the London School of Economics and Political Science, that helped towards funding my almost annual visits to Hong Kong since the mid-1980s. The Woodrow Wilson Center in Washington, DC, kindly provided me with excellent facilities as a Guest Scholar in April 1995 to enquire into American perspectives on the Hong Kong question.

Introduction
The challenge and the opportunity

When China resumes sovereignty of Hong Kong on 1 July 1997 it will begin an undertaking of enormous significance for the future of China itself. The way in which it lives up to its promises and legal obligations will not only determine the fate of the former British colony and its six million inhabitants, but it will also shape the evolution of China's political identity and its integration into the international community. In other words, the return of Hong Kong provides China with a unique opportunity to adapt to the special challenges it faces both at home and abroad. It is not only a question of whether Hong Kong can continue to flourish as a major international centre or whether it will sink back to being a relatively parochial entrepôt for Guangdong Province, but rather a question of determining China's own future.

CHINA'S POTENTIAL GAINS AND LOSSES

If China's communist leaders were able to honour the pledge of allowing Hong Kong to maintain its rule of law and basic freedoms that have underlaid its unique success as a centre of capitalism and international finance, China would continue to benefit from the enormous economic contribution the territory makes to its modernisation and its deepening engagement with the international economy, and the beneficial political consequences would be immense. Such a display of tolerance for an autonomous Hong Kong would consolidate its new relations with the Chinese communities outside China, strengthen Beijing's stance regarding Taiwan, reduce anxieties in Southeast Asia, ease China's relations with the USA and Japan, enhance the process of China's integration within the Asia-Pacific region, and improve China's international standing generally.

China's new leaders – the successors to Deng Xiaoping – face their first big political test in managing the transfer of sovereignty in 1997. In the absence of a new 'strong man', the uneasy collective leadership would greatly strengthen its political standing and self-confidence if it were able to bring back Hong Kong into the embrace of the motherland without shattering the basis of its fragile identity. By going on to show that the much proclaimed concept of 'one country two systems' could actually work in practice, the new leaders would demonstrate unprecedented statesmanship.

The concept, first put forward in the late 1970s with Taiwan in mind, envisions that Hong Kong could flourish for at least fifty years amid prosperity and stability as a democratic self-governing capitalist enclave under the sovereignty of a socialist China that is still led by its communist party. There is no precedent for such an exercise. Historians may point to the old imperial practice in China of allowing small groups of outsiders with alien customs to be largely self-administering autonomous units, but their autonomy was always limited by the need to act within the framework of Chinese law and by the tolerance of the Chinese authorities – it was not theirs by right. Arguably, the treaty ports in which foreigners exercised extra-territorial rights as a result of the unequal treaties of the nineteenth century may also be considered as precedents of a kind, but these were wrested from the Chinese state by superior force of arms. Moreover, there is no experience of a communist state voluntarily conceding from a position of undoubted overwhelming power that such an enclave should come into existence. The Autonomous Regions in China or the Republics of the former Soviet Union, in practice, were under the tight control of the central communist authorities. In this case, the autonomy promised to Hong Kong has derived not simply from an act of state that could easily be revoked, but has been established by an international treaty with the former colonial power and confirmed by a kind of a covenant with the local Chinese Hong Kong people in the shape of a Basic Law that has been ratified by the sovereign body in Beijing, the National People's Congress (NPC). China's leaders and the Chinese Communist Party (CCP) will be required to refrain from exercising their long established practice of seeking to control and administer nearly every facet of life within the territory of their sovereign state. This administrative impulse, it should be noted, is all the stronger for having been deeply ingrained in the traditions of Chinese bureaucracy down the ages.

Simply by leaving the people of Hong Kong to administer

themselves and enjoy their existing freedoms and way of life in accordance with the law, China's leaders would demonstrate unusual tolerance and a remarkable capacity to have understood a great deal about what has made Hong Kong so successful. Even if China's leaders were not fully conversant with the reasons for the territory's success, the sheer importance of recognising the need for non-interference and for preventing the practices of the mainland spilling across the border would be immense. A member of the seven man Standing Committee of the Politburo (technically the highest political authority in China), Li Ruihuan gave a remarkable talk in which he conceded that the Chinese leaders lacked a proper understanding of what were the important factors that enabled Hong Kong to be such a successful commercial centre. His address to a visiting delegation from Hong Kong in March 1995 was published in full by one of the communist newspapers in Hong Kong.[1] He likened the Chinese takeover to the case of a lady who had agreed to sell a hundred-year-old Yi Xiang teapot that was famous for the quality of the tea that it poured. Unbeknown to her, its quality derived from the residue that had accumulated on the inside of the pot. In her eagerness to prepare the pot for the purchaser she polished it and removed the said residue. When the purchaser came to redeem it he pronounced the pot valueless. Unfortunately, unlike the Party General Secretary Jiang Zemin, or the Premier Li Peng, Li Ruihuan has no functional responsibility for the conduct of policy towards Hong Kong.

If Li Ruihuan's warnings were heeded and the special character of Hong Kong not rubbed out, the benefits would be great indeed. It would also suggest that the leaders had recognised some of the fundamentals about the operation of the international economy that would portend well for China's increasing engagement with the international community. It could, for example, ease China's entry into the World Trade Organization (WTO) and increase foreign investment in China. Moreover, by tolerating on their doorstep a Hong Kong that can enjoy 'a high degree of autonomy' (as promised in the 1984 treaty with Britain), China's leaders would confound the doubters and, for the short term, enhance political stability at home. By demonstrating a deeper appreciation of the significance of the rule of law than has been shown so far, China's leaders would do much to strengthen its role within China itself.

Conversely, were China's leaders to fail to carry out their promise to implement their scheme for Hong Kong of 'one country two systems', Deng's successors would not only fail to benefit from the substantive new economic opportunities, but they would materially damage China's interests in general and those of Chinese communism in particular. The first step would be the actual transfer of sovereignty on 1 July 1997. If this were to be mishandled by the new leaders, confidence in their capacity to carry out openness (*kaifeng*) as an integral part of economic reform and development would decline. The reforms would take on a more conservative hue and the fault lines in China's political economy would widen, leading to incalculable consequences for China's economic modernisation that, in turn, could undermine the delicate balances holding the country together. Amid a sense of deeper vulnerability at home, China's leaders would address the world in more truculent terms. Once the policy of 'one country two systems' were to be shown to have failed in Hong Kong, China's leaders would no longer be able to offer it as a viable basis on which to call for the peaceful reunification with Taiwan. Force would be left as the only credible option.

Japan and especially the USA would be greatly troubled by the damage to Hong Kong and would be anxious about the fate of Taiwan. At the minimum they would seek to strengthen the resolve of its people and to bolster its defences. The Southeast Asian countries would find less merit in their policy of engagement with China, and the various Chinese communities in the region would have to readjust their ties with the land of their fathers. China would probably retreat into a new kind of isolationism which might threaten the stability of the Asia-Pacific region as a whole.

CHINA'S DOMESTIC TRAVAILS

It should be recognised that the return of Hong Kong to Chinese sovereignty will pose many problems to China itself. If the actual process of the transfer of sovereignty could be successfully managed, Hong Kong could then pose further challenges to the Chinese communist government. In particular, it would serve as an attractive model for all those in China who seek the benefits of greater legality and increased democratic accountability. There might be those in Shanghai, for example, who might question why Hong Kong had become so much more successful than Shanghai itself in the second half of the twentieth century when, in the previous fifty years or more, it was Hong Kong that was the relative backwater. In other words, a Hong Kong that flourished within the framework of 'one country two systems' could become dangerously subversive of the communist system in China by its demonstration effect alone, even if none of its citizens actively intervened in Chinese affairs. Clearly, the extent of the danger that the Hong Kong model might pose to communist rule in China would depend to a considerable extent upon conditions in China. In particular, much would turn on the capacity of the leaders and the communist party to preside over continued prosperity and to meet the enormous challenges that rapid economic development have thrown up.

The resolution of the future of Hong Kong is being determined at a time of great moment in Chinese history. China is in the process of fundamental change and its future direction is uncertain. The country confronts immense problems that do not lend themselves to easy solution. Despite (or perhaps because of) the phenomenal economic growth rates of nearly ten per cent per year since 1979, the country suffers from endemic inflation that is in part the result of having to finance bloated and inefficient state-owned enterprises that employ 100 million people – a large proportion of the urban work force – who cannot be made redundant for fear of social unrest. There are immense disparities between the coastal and interior provinces and between the urban and rural areas that have resulted in a migration of as many as 150 million people from the countryside into the cities. Crime is widespread, social tensions are high and corruption is pervasive in the ruling communist party. Communist ideology has lost such appeal as it once had and, in the absence of a culture of legality, it has not been replaced by the rule of law. Authority is exercised in the name of ensuring stability and providing for rapid economic growth. The spectre of the disorder in Russia allied to traditional fears of anarchic chaos (*luan*) has limited the challenge to the regime since the killings of Tiananmen of 4 June 1989 and the challenge of dissenters has been met with repressive force.

China is poised uneasily between the remnants of the old command economic system and the emerging new market system without having established fully effective macro-economic means of controlling the two. The core of its traditional economic and political power is vested in the old state sector which is managed through complex systems of administrative directives. This sector accounts for the bulk of heavy industry and the major utilities. Its proponents regard it as central to the operation of the economy as a whole. Yet the high economic growth since 1979 has been provided by the non-state-owned parts of the economy, as can be seen from the fact that in 1978 it only accounted for about five per cent of the value of the country's industrial production and in 1994 it accounted for about fifty per cent. In the course of this change, the centre has shed considerable economic powers to the provinces and to local enterprises that have released centrifugal forces that challenge the integrity of the Chinese state. China has yet to demonstrate a capacity to exercise macro-economic control through economic levers.

More difficulties could be listed such as those of environmental degradation, disaffected ethnic minorities, problems in agriculture and so on, but enough has been said to show that, despite its so-called economic miracle, the Chinese state is beset with structural problems with no ready solution to hand. These may be seen as compounded by the political succession taking place from the generation of the revolutionary founding fathers to that of bureaucratic leaders who were hand picked by their elders. Since institutional legal authority is still weak at the highest levels of politics, supreme authority in China still tends to be personal. Those who will have to steer China through its immense problems and into the next century will lack the immediate authority of a Mao or a Deng who commanded respect simultaneously from leaders in the army, the state bureaucracy and the communist party. Since the new generation of Jiang Zemin, Li Peng, Qiao Shi etc. represent the elite trained by the Soviet Union in the 1950s, they and their kind must be considered as transitional that in time will be replaced by a younger generation more in tune with the technocratic needs of a market economy. Thus, the political succession in China must also be considered as a prolonged and uncertain process.

THE NEW MARITIME DIMENSION

From a broader perspective, China may be seen as being in the process of a deep historical change of gigantic proportions from being essentially an inward looking continental country to an outward looking maritime one. It no longer faces major security problems from the north or from inner Asia. According to its military planners, China's principal security requirements are to acquire sufficient modern naval and air capabilities to uphold its interests in the maritime regions to the east and the south. Since the mid-1980s, China's armed forces have emphasised the need to become a more professional force, able to carry out combined operations and equipped with the latest technology. The sources for modernity whether in terms of management know-how, advanced technology, investment or access to markets lie beyond the blue seas and oceans. In so far as the Chinese seek to modernise in order to enable their people to become prosperous and their country to become a strong global power, they cannot but deepen their maritime orientation. Since the new course was begun in 1978, the economies of the coastal belt of provinces have far outshone those of the interior. In the ten-year period, 1984–1994, when the GDP more than doubled, the proportion accounted by the coastal provinces increased from 50 to 57 per cent. There has been a shift of population towards the coastal region as the better educated have gravitated there from the interior and up to 150 million people have left the land in search of better prospects. The majority of these have moved to the cities, particularly those of the coastal regions. The coastal regions have been the primary sources of propelling economic growth. They attract most foreign investment and have become important factors in providing continuing dynamism to the economies of the Asia-Pacific as a whole. In this sense, they also play a critical role in helping to integrate the Chinese economy with those of its East Asian neighbours.

Those who may be called the maritime Chinese of Hong Kong, Taiwan and of Southeast Asia and beyond have contributed mightily to the economic modernisation of their ancestral land, especially in Guangdong and other maritime provinces from which they or their forbears had left. Without their factories, management and market skills, it is inconceivable that mainland Chinese would have been able to produce goods of sufficient high quality and fashion appeal so as to penetrate western markets so quickly after embarking on the policies of modernisation in December 1978. Hong Kong itself has been central to this exercise. Within a short space of time its factories were rebuilt across the border so that, by the early 1980s, three million out of its four million workforce were residents of Guangdong employed in factories located there. Hong Kong has also been the conduit for most of the economic interactions with the mainland of the other centres of maritime China. Since 1978, more than seventy-five per cent of the direct foreign investment in China (estimated by the end of 1994 as a cumulative total of $100 billion) has come from or through Hong Kong. It is that investment coupled with the other foreign related enterprises in China (many, if not most, derived from Hong Kong) that has provided the base for the bulk of China's manufactured exports. In other words, Hong Kong has been a key pivot in China's economic modernisation so far.

Hong Kong and the maritime Chinese which traditionally were on the periphery of the Chinese state have become more important in terms of China's political culture as well as in terms of economics. China's political identity is changing even as it is led by the communist party. Just as the maritime dimensions of China are being accentuated, so are the communist claims to have established a 'New China' in 1949 being eroded. The socialist ideals of those early years have long gone. In the 1950s and 1960s mainland Chinese used to claim superiority as adherents of a socialist creed who were building a selfless new order for the public good. The people of Hong Kong and, indeed, most Chinese overseas were dismissed as people who lived in a capitalist society driven by greed and the exploitation of the many by the few. Their only saving grace might have been a degree of patriotic sentiments which would have been expressed by a measure of deference to their mainland compatriots. During the Cultural Revolution, even that saving grace was denied as they and their mainland relations were denounced as dangerously polluted by their foreign connections. By the late 1970s, however, the mainlanders had become disillusioned with Maoist dogma and disoriented to discover the vastly superior economic accomplishments of the East Asian economies and of Hong Kong in particular, whom they had previously disparaged. They were damaged from within by the excesses of class struggle and by relative economic failure compared to the East Asian capitalist economies.

For the present, it is the economic achievement associated with the programme of modernisation that has highlighted the role of the commercial periphery. The variety of the different centres of localist culture, both inside the mainland and beyond, have pinpointed the inadequacies of the earlier communist attempt to establish a unitary version under its monopoly. Because of the continuing predominance of communist party rule and the pervasiveness of so-called 'money worship' on the mainland, intellectual discussion of the possible political futures of China has tended to be stifled. It is in this context that in the 1990s Hong Kong has emerged as an intellectual centre for analysis of the different claims for asserting new senses of Chinese identity in addition to its long-standing role as the crossroads for exchanges between different Chinese communities.

THE CONFLICT OF CULTURES

It is, however, very difficult for China's leaders to take such a dispassionate view of Hong Kong and its significance. Not only does much of this challenge the basis for communist party rule on the mainland, but the cultural divide between them and their compatriots of Hong Kong is wide and deep. No Chinese leader, who has only experienced forty-five years of communist rule where everything has been politicised and made subordinate to the dictates of the Party Centre, can appreciate the significance of the free market let alone the operation of freedom under the law. Even the idea of an independent judiciary is alien. As one senior communist official asked me rhetorically in the summer of 1990 when discussing the question of Hong Kong's Court of Final Appeal: 'What happens if the judges get it wrong?' Few Chinese leaders may be said to understand the importance of the rule of law for a capitalist economy, and fewer still may be said to appreciate the concept of governmental accountability. All of these, however, are central to the way of life in Hong Kong where people air a whole variety of views, enjoy the freedom of like-minded people to associate where and when they please, protected by an independent judiciary and administered by a professional and efficient civil service that is not subject to the orders of a party cabal. It is under these terms that the Hong Kong Chinese have laboured and their entrepreneurial skills flourished and brought about the miracle that is Hong Kong.

The outlook of China's leaders is also conditioned by their country's past Confucian traditions and lofty mandarin rule. The disdain for the foreigner and for foreign ways is only matched by the contempt for Chinese who have subjected themselves to the foreigners' yoke. To this day, most Chinese are imbued with the nationalist sense of outrage by the century of shame and humiliation inflicted upon their country by the West from the 1840s to the 1940s. That, of course, started with the Treaty of Nanking by which Hong Kong island was ceded to the British. From this perspective it should follow that the overwhelming majority of patriotic Hong Kong Chinese should welcome the return to the motherland after all these years of colonial servitude. Not surprisingly, at no point in the prolonged negotiations with the British has the Chinese side allowed Hong Kong Chinese to be represented independently. All attempts by the British to bring along such persons to represent the viewpoint of the local people have been curtly dismissed. They have been allowed to participate only as members of the British team.

Hong Kong itself was reborn after the Second World War and the Chinese civil war. The population of some 600,000 that was re-established in the aftermath of the Japanese surrender in August 1945 was rapidly augmented by an influx of refugees from the Chinese civil war so that, by 1951, it reached 2.5 million. Among them were several thousand entrepreneurs from Shanghai who were able to transform Hong Kong into a light industrial manufacturing base as a result of the economic embargo that the Americans imposed upon China upon the outbreak of the Korean War in June 1950. Up until that point the territory had largely been an entrepôt for southern China – a relative backwater overshadowed by Shanghai. At this stage, Hong Kong was made up of mainly four groups of Chinese: the Cantonese speakers originally from Guangdong Province who constituted the vast majority; the traditional clans of the farming people in the New Territories; the Chiu Chiow (mainly fisherfolk from Eastern Guang-dong); and Hakka people (originally northerners who had come south several centuries before and who had never been assimilated by the southerners), also mainly from Guangdong; as well as the several thousand people who had fled from Shanghai.

Initially, these refugees lived mainly as squatters and only after disasters from fire and flooding did the government eventually ensure that they were offered rudimentary housing. As refugees, they were content to accept British rule and concentrate upon earning a living. A few became highly successful and were accepted into the British-led elite. The British and the other expatriates accounted for only about two per cent of the population, but they determined the system of government and that of the economy. This was not challenged by the refugee population which was pleased to be left alone to focus on hard work while being free of communist control. They had little commitment to Hong Kong *per se* as they had come from elsewhere on the mainland which they still tended to regard as their ancestral home. Their children, however, who grew to maturity from the mid-1970s onwards were fully committed to Hong Kong as the only home they had known. It is from that time that the beginning of an assertion of a distinctive cultural and political identity for Hong Kong can be traced. This was associated with the growth of a middle-class professional stratum. They tended to be better educated than their parents, but based on a peculiar mix of British and Hong Kong Chinese educational approaches. They began to take a greater interest in cultural pursuits than their parents and they sought better means of government accountability. By the time of the Sino-British Joint Declaration of 1984 that envisioned a future autonomy based on democratic accountability, there had emerged in Hong Kong a growing middle class that had asserted a new identity for Hong Kong and that sought to participate more in government.

At this point, few educated Hong Kong Chinese had much knowledge of the communist north. Until recent years, most people had been content to work, make money and get on with their lives under British law and a British inspired civil service free from communist rule. For the civil service and most professional people in Hong Kong, the Communist north was *terra incognita* about which it was not necessary nor perhaps healthy to be closely informed. Thus, the two coexisted side by side with little knowledge of or sympathy with the other, although each played important roles for the other.

If divisions existed between the Hong Kong Chinese and their 'compatriots' to the north, the cultural divide between China and Britain was deeper still. Thus, despite their common interest in reaching an accommodation about achieving a smooth transfer of sovereignty in 1997, they have been too separated by their divergent political cultures to do so, even though they have been negotiating more or less continuously in one form or another since 1979. Conscious of the depth of the divide between them and of China's lack of understanding of the workings of Hong Kong, the British first proposed that they be allowed to continue to administer Hong Kong after the retrocession of sovereignty. That only served to provoke the fiercely nationalistic Chinese who had never regarded sovereignty as simply a question of legal status. They denied the implication that as Chinese they did not know how to govern Chinese people living on a territory that was rightfully a part of the motherland. And for good measure they suspected the British of harbouring ulterior commercial and political purposes. These early misunderstandings and signs of distrust have bedeviled the negotiations ever since. They may end up causing the transfer of sovereignty to be handled disastrously, even though it is in the manifest interest of all three parties that the transfer be handled smoothly and successfully.

DIVISIONS WITHIN EACH CULTURE OVER THE NEGOTIATIONS

In fact, the processes of negotiations and accommodations have been affected by the clashes of three political cultures each of which, additionally, has become divided over the principal issues. On the Chinese side, where traditional and Communist approaches have interacted to produce deep suspicions and misperceptions of the British position as well as to engender immense difficulties in understanding how Hong Kong works and the character of its emerging political system, new divisions have recently appeared. On the one side, the economic centrists (with a powerful base in the remnants of the command economy organisations) set great store by the state-owned enterprises and seek to control and direct foreign investment away from the coast to the interior and to infrastructure projects and, accordingly, would like to limit Hong Kong's economic and cultural influence. On the other side are the less well-organised groups with interest in building the rule of law, maintaining the open door, deepening marketisation and continuing the development of the coastal regions as a matter of high priority, who generally favour the continuation of Hong Kong's current role.

With its legal and trading traditions and a deep entrenchment in the norms of European politics and diplomacy, the British side has also been divided. On the one hand are those who favour, above all, reaching agreements with the Chinese despite their short-fall in terms of democratic ideals, even if that should mean doing so over the objections of Hong Kong politicians. On the other hand are those who argue that the agreement of the Hong Kong people is necessary and that they should be provided with institutions that do not militate in advance against the prospect of the exercise of autonomy after the transfer of sovereignty, even if by doing so cooperation with the Chinese should break down.

Hong Kong itself, which is increasingly subject to awful polarising pressures between those said to be pro-Chinese and those accused of being pro-British, is also divided. On one side are the Chinese businessmen with their traditional family-oriented ways of organising their business and conducting deals, who are less impressed by the claims of the necessity of the law and democracy in Hong Kong. On the other are the professionals and other members of the middle class, the generation who came to maturity in the late 1970s and who have contributed greatly to giving the territory its unique culture and status as an international financial centre. They have little contact with mainland China and are anxious to establish a workable democracy on the territory before the return to Chinese sovereignty.

PROBLEMATIC NEGOTIATIONS

The clashes between these cultures have made the Sino-British negotiations unusually acrimonious and difficult. The Chinese side may be said to have held the whip hand as Hong Kong could not be defended from a determined Chinese attempt to take it over. The British laboured in the knowledge that at any point the Chinese could have simply imposed a unilateral solution. But China's leaders nevertheless recognised the enormous advantages of a negotiated settlement that would allow as much continuity as possible to this important asset to the Chinese economy and that would stand China in good stead in its attempts to persuade Taiwan to reunify with the mainland. On the British side, it was long accepted that there could be no future for Hong Kong without China's consent. Thus, it has been in the interests of both sides to reach a negotiated settlement, recognising that this was the best means of safeguarding the territory's stability, prosperity and the way of life that has underpinned them.

The very different British and Chinese cultures, historical experiences, political systems and diplomatic styles have resulted in misunderstandings and misperceptions. The British side has been pursuing (perhaps uniquely in British foreign policy) a diplomacy based on morality and a degree of altruism for which it has been willing to sacrifice economic interests. Ministers and senior officials may be said to be motivated by guilt at handing over this last major colony to a dictatorship whose brutality was openly displayed in the Tiananmen killings of 4 June 1989 while simultaneously denying its 3.5 million British passport holders the right of residence in Britain because of opposition in Parliament. Consequently, they have felt and continue to feel a deep moral obligation to reach the best settlement available for the people of Hong Kong so as to enable them to continue to exercise a high degree of autonomy from a regime that the British are convinced still does not understand what makes Hong Kong work.

The Chinese side, however, deeply conscious of Britain's imperial past and of the rapacious interests that first drove it to seize the territory in the nineteenth century, has not accepted that Britain has changed colour and that it is genuinely motivated by a sense of obligation to the people there. Still less is it believed in Beijing that Britain can represent the interests of what are, after all, the Chinese people of Hong Kong. In the view of China's leaders, Britain's principal interest has been and continues to be to make money from Hong Kong. From the outset, Deng Xiaoping instructed his negotiators to 'watch those British, lest they abscond with the capital'.[2] Additionally, in the aftermath of 4 June 1989, China's leaders suspected that Britain was associated with the USA in what they perceived as concerted policies of trying to change China's domestic system through a process of ideological pressure and capitalist penetration that they have called 'peaceful evolution'. They have also been concerned lest Britain should try to leave a legacy of trouble behind in Hong Kong so as to contribute to the destabilisation of China in accordance with what they perceive as an American determination to prevent China from attaining its rightful place in the world as a modern global power. More generally, China's leaders have tended to assess British policy in terms of the fluidities of power politics and their sense of British interests as a relatively declining power. British protestations of honourable intentions are regarded at best as baffling and, more usually, as hypocrisy masking ulterior motives.

THE STRUCTURE AND ORGANISATION OF THE NEGOTIATIONS

Allied to these perceptual problems, the structure of the negotiations and the ways in which the two sides organised themselves for the negotiations have also been sources of trouble. The negotiations were structured so as to involve only China and Britain as the two sovereign powers. The question of involving Hong Kong representation as the third party that was most directly involved was dismissed by the Chinese as an unacceptable 'three legged stool'. But this became increasingly problematic as Hong Kong acquired a degree of democracy and accountability in the late 1980s and early 1990s. In 1991, the point was reached when an agreement between the Chinese and British governments was thrown out by the semi-democratised Legislative Council of Hong Kong. The agreement was suspended and in the end another agreement on the subject had to be negotiated between the two sovereign powers four years later in 1995. By this time, even the Chinese side recognised the significance of Hong Kong's legislative procedures as it undertook to help towards the passing of the necessary bill. At this late stage it was accepted by the British as part of the compromise with Beijing that the Court could not be convened before the transfer of sovereignty on 1 July 1997.

The Chinese side of the negotiations was organised in ways that contributed to the difficulties. From Beijing's point of view Hong Kong was neither a domestic nor a foreign issue and as a result it had not developed a bureaucratic machinery to deal with it. Until he became inactive at the end of 1994, Deng Xiaoping took a personal interest in the negotiations and made the final decisions as well as providing overall guidance to the negotiators. These came from organisations that had few, if any, links with other Chinese bureaucracies and that, apart from the Foreign Ministry, were not headed by people of the first rank. Moreover, the Hong Kong Branch of the New China News Agency (NCNA) and the Hong Kong and Macao Affairs Office (HKMAO, who handle much of the details of the negotiations) have no bureaucratic interest in how the Special Administrative Region (SAR) of Hong Kong will be administered after the transfer of sovereignty in 1997, since at that point the newly created SAR will be administered by a Chinese appointed Chief Executive. Meanwhile, China's extensive economic interests in the territory, including those of many provincial and governmental agencies as well as organisations such as the Bank of China, China Resources etc., that have a good working knowledge of the territory have no formal mechanisms available by which their interest and expertise can influence the negotiators. Once Deng himself became too infirm to give active leadership, a vacuum developed in China's handling of Hong Kong affairs and a danger appeared that it might become hostage to the politics of succession in Beijing.

On the British side, negotiations have also been handled by a relatively small team of negotiators drawn from the Foreign and Commonwealth Office subject to the overall leadership of ministers. Since the Hong Kong issue was relatively marginal to British politics except for pressure to prevent the possibility of significant immigration, the ministers and negotiators were able to resist pressures from British companies and the British media in order to pursue what they regarded as their obligations to Hong Kong. The former have argued against damaging economic interests with China and the latter have urged for upholding high democratic principles regardless of Chinese objections. Conscious of China's superior bargaining position that could allow it to impose a unilateral solution, British negotiators pursued a narrow line trying to provide for a post-1997 framework that would allow for autonomy and satisfy the people of Hong Kong *without* bringing about a complete breakdown with the Chinese side. In view of these difficulties, it is perhaps remarkable how much has been agreed between all the parties even though there are still a number of crucial steps ahead.

THE PROBLEMS OF TRANSITION

In 1992 the British government, in keeping with its colonial tradition, appointed a senior politician, Chris Patten, to be the last governor to take charge of the difficult final years leading to the transfer of sovereignty.[3] His proposals and the manner of their announcement without prior consultation in October 1992 to extend the franchise for elections in Hong Kong were rejected with much acrimony by the Chinese side and they served to intensify its suspicions that the British government's departure from the previous practice of appointing seasoned diplomats was part of a broader scheme to create trouble for China. The fact that the governments of Australia, Canada and especially the USA publicly gave their warm support to Patten's proposals tended to confirm suspicions in Beijing that the proposals were part of an international scheme to encourage Hong Kong to become more independent as a centre of democracy aimed at subverting the Chinese political system. It took another two and a half years before Sino-British relations began to show definite signs of improvement and it was not until three years had passed that the Chinese Foreign Minister, Qian Qichen, visited London to herald a new period of better cooperation between the two sides.

Even if Sino-British cooperation was to prove more satisfactory in Patten's last two years than they were in his first two years as governor, the final period of transition to the transfer of sovereignty on midnight 30 June 1997 will still be fraught with difficulties on the Chinese side. Having postponed all their major decisions about the administration of the SAR to the last 18 months without preparing even a rough blueprint of what they have in mind, the Chinese authorities are confronted with several problems. The Preparatory Committee selected by January 1996 will be required to nominate an election committee drawn from all circles within Hong Kong that will have to choose a Chief Executive who will have to satisfy the near impossible criteria of having lived for at least twenty years in the territory, being respected by the international community, enjoying the confidence of the bulk of the people of Hong Kong and who is also trusted by the Chinese leaders. Once selected in 1996, that person will have to work closely with the governor and the senior civil service for a year or so in order to develop a good understanding of the job. Since Beijing is pledged to form a provisional Legislative Council on 1 July 1997 to replace the one elected in 1995, it is unclear how the putative Chief Executive will deal with the latter as it continues to perform functions central to the governance of the territory.

Meanwhile, there will be many areas of importance to the future of Hong Kong that have been delayed largely by Chinese procrastination in the negotiations in the aftermath of the proposals put forward by Governor Patten in October 1992. These will have to be dealt with in an unseemly haste. By this stage, the question of sustaining the confidence of the people of Hong Kong will be a Chinese problem. In their zest to constrain the more outspoken democrats in Hong Kong, China's leaders will have to take care not to alienate the many professionals in the territory, not a few of whom hold foreign passports and have the right of abode elsewhere. The establishment of a provisional Legislative Council is fraught with problems that could be very destabilising to a territory that depends so much on confidence for the exercise of its functions as an international centre and, indeed, as an entrepôt too. The Chinese authorities will have to demonstrate unusual sensitivity in the last eighteen months before the handover if they are to avoid the flight of capital, a collapse of the property market and a large exodus of the professionals and the elite.

1997 AND BEYOND

In 1994 the Chinese authorities set up at the entrance to the Museum of Revolutionary History in the heart of Tiananmen Square a huge clock to count down the days, hours, minutes and seconds to the return of sovereignty of Hong Kong. This was done as a public reminder to the people of Hong Kong that they were due to be embraced by the motherland under the leadership of the Chinese Communist Party before too long. But it has since been appreciated that the seconds tick by for Beijing too. By placing the clock in a place of such symbolic meaning China's leaders have elevated the significance of the transfer of sovereignty to a matter of national pride and significance.

China's leaders may be tempted to mark the occasion by placing their particular stamp on the new order that will prevail in the Hong Kong SAR, but national prestige would be sorely damaged if that were to cause an exodus by the tens and hundreds of thousands of those with the capacity to leave. Indeed, more than prestige would be at stake if, in the process, Hong Kong itself were to experience a massive drain of confidence. Clearly, there are no rational grounds for believing that China's leaders would choose to act in such a self-defeating way.

A dire outcome cannot be dismissed, however, partly because of the actual difficulties of managing the process of the transition and partly because of the stresses and strains of the divisions within the Chinese hierarchy. The former could be eased through better cooperative relations with the outgoing British administration and there are grounds for some optimism about that despite the conflicting signals. However, the impact of the political divisions within China is less predictable.

The Chinese Communist Party will find 1997 to be a particularly difficult year as it is scheduled to convene the first national Party congress after the likely death of Deng Xiaoping. That is a time when the ranking of the different leaders has to be settled and revealed in public. A new Central Committee will be chosen along with an authoritative account of the previous five years laid out together with an outline of the programme for the next five years. This will be an occasion for the different personalities and forces within the Party to vie for position and to struggle to have their particular approaches to China's problems legitimised. The build-up to the congress is usually a testing time of jockeying for position and of argumentation about the drafting of the Party's programmatic documents. Since congresses are normally held in September and October, the reversion of sovereignty of Hong Kong on 1 July 1997 will occur as the manoeuvring over the congress intensifies. The transfer of sovereignty will inevitably become caught up in domestic politics in ways that cannot be predicted and that will inevitably contribute to the uncertainties.

Among the many divisions and fault lines evident in Chinese politics, reference has already been made to that between the more conservative centralists – called 'the browns' (from the colour of the Yellow River) – and the more enthusiastic reformers and open-doorists – 'the blues' (from the colour of the ocean). The latter constitute a powerful force that may be regarded as advocating policies broadly favourable to the continuation of Hong Kong in its present form. Not only do they promote the cause of continuing high economic growth and further reforms along market lines, but they also favour more openness and the strengthening of the rule of law.

The former, by contrast, fear for the future of socialism in China and seek to protect the old state-owned enterprises, control foreign investment, and limit the alleged anarchy of the free market and its corrupting tendencies. Accordingly, Hong Kong is seen by this group as a challenge rather than an opportunity – as a place whose influence upon China should be curtailed and better directed.

The international community and especially the USA may be said to have a role to play in affecting the future of Hong Kong. By pursuing a constructive rather than a confrontational approach to China, the outside world would be less likely to evoke a truculent nationalist response that could stifle the voices of 'the blues'. The West would have to find ways of balancing the need to uphold the cause of human rights in Hong Kong with encouraging the observance of commercial and contractual law. It should ideally seek to provide the Chinese with incentives to live up to their obligations while also seeking counter measures to demonstrate resolve to stand up for the interest of the international community in the continuation of Hong Kong's way of life and in the international role associated with it. Given the disarray in the West about the pursuit of purposive foreign policy, it may be too much to expect that such a carefully calculated policy could be carried out. But it would make a difference if those who demand that respect for human rights be given absolute priority in the determination and the execution of policies to be applied towards China, and Hong Kong should at least give pause to consider the wider issues at stake.

As argued earlier, China is in the process of undergoing a series of massive transformations: from being a continental country to becoming one with a greater maritime orientation; from being a command economy to becoming a market one; from being a totalitarian state to evolving into a more pluralist one; from being a lawless state to one that is acquiring the rudiments of the rule of law; and from being a unitary state to one that is developing federal characteristics. The retrocession of sovereignty over Hong Kong provides China and its people the opportunity to ease their transition that could otherwise be painful and traumatic not only for China, but also for its neighbours and, indeed, for the international community as a whole.

This book will be organised so as to address the problems of the nature of the challenges and opportunities that arise for China from the reversion of sovereignty in 1997. This is not to downgrade the significance of the fate of the six million residents of Hong Kong, nor to overlook the importance of Britain's moral obligations to them and their welfare. Rather, the intention is to highlight the problems and opportunities that arise from the perspectives of the Chinese authorities. The importance of that in shaping the future of Hong Kong can hardly be exaggerated, yet it has been relatively neglected in the extensive writings about the territory and the transfer of sovereignty to China.

The book will start with an evaluation of the economic importance of Hong Kong and of its significance as the centre of so-called Greater China involving also Taiwan, the two adjacent coastal provinces of Guangdong and Fujian, and, according to some accounts, the wider ethnic Chinese communities in Southeast Asia. The arguments sketched out above about the political significance of the territory will be developed further.

Chapter 2 will explore further the problems arising from the clash of cultures with particular reference to the evolution of the coexistence that has prevailed over Hong Kong since the establishment of the communist state in China in 1949. Chapter 3 will trace the evolution of the relatively successful, but always difficult, Sino-British negotiations in which the clash of cultures will be shown to have led to repeated misunderstandings and misperceptions.

The problems of managing the transition towards the transfer of sovereignty will be considered in Chapter 4 and will focus primarily upon the dilemmas on the Chinese side, but will also discuss the problems as seen from within Hong Kong. The book will conclude with an assessment of the wider implications of the reversion of sovereignty with reference to both the domestic issues involving the evolution of China itself and to the international repercussions.

Chapter 1

The significance of Hong Kong

In the half century from 1945 to 1995 Hong Kong has been transformed from a derelict backwater to become the eighth largest trading economy in the world. When the Japanese surrendered in 1945, the 600,000 inhabitants were on the verge of starvation; fifty years later the six million people of Hong Kong enjoy on average a higher income than the population of Britain: Hong Kong ranked seventeenth in the world in terms of GDP per person.[1] In the late 1980s, Hong Kong overtook Rotterdam to become the world's busiest container port. It is Asia's leading financial centre and the third in the world after London and New York. Such significance as is usually attached to Hong Kong stems to a considerable extent from these economic achievements that have enabled it to play a major role in the international economy of East Asia and a crucial role in the rapid economic development of China itself. But as a plethora of recent books have shown, the significance of Hong Kong extends far beyond the realm of economics.[2]

The purpose here, however, is not to attempt to describe the significance of Hong Kong in its own right, but rather to attempt to do so with Chinese interests in mind, particularly in view of the impending reversion of sovereignty. Economics is crucial here too, but so are politics, culture and the relations with Taiwan. Hong Kong is also at the centre of a complex web of relations linking China with the so-called Overseas Chinese, and it is also at the heart of 'Greater China' – the economic entity that integrates southern China with Hong Kong and Taiwan. More broadly, Hong Kong plays a vital role in providing China with a gateway to the economies of the Asia-Pacific and beyond that to the global international economy. Although this has not been generally recognised, Hong Kong has become an important element in China's foreign relations as a whole.

It has also played an important role as the agent of the modernisation of the country through investment, transfers of technology, management, financial skills, access to western markets etc. By the same token, as the agent of modernity and marketisation Hong Kong also constitutes a challenge to the traditional command economy and to the centres of administrative and ideological authority of the communist-led state.

Many factors have contributed to the success of Hong Kong including its geographical location and its possession of the best deep water port on the Chinese coast. But the most important have been the administrative structure and the rule of law provided by the British which have enabled the Chinese people of Hong Kong to improve their living conditions by working hard and to expand their entrepreneurial flair and, in time, to develop their professional skills. These key elements allied to an efficient infrastructure, sound finances and low taxes, and a free port that have enabled goods and capital to flow in and out freely have given an edge to Hong Kong over most other business centres throughout the world. Hong Kong's achievements have been realised without subsidised loans and against a background of instability and turmoil in China. China was fortunate to have had such a place flourishing on its doorstep when it embarked in 1978 on the long and rocky road of economic reform and openness.

From Beijing's perspective, the undoubted economic significance of Hong Kong is tempered by the nationalist pride in at last re-establishing sovereignty over the first territory to have been lost to foreign imperialists in the century of shame and humiliation that began with the Opium Wars of 1839–1842. The intensity of the nationalistic sentiment about the prospect of regaining sovereignty was nonetheless keen, even though the Chinese side could have regained Hong Kong more or less at any time of its choosing since 1949. Indeed, the British negotiators in the early 1980s were surprised by the depth of the Chinese feelings on the matter. As one of the most senior people on the British side remarked, 'Deng Xiaoping was determined to take [Hong Kong] back into full Chinese sovereignty even if it meant taking it back as a barren rock'.[3] For China's leaders, the retrocession of sovereignty is also part of re-establishing the unity of the Chinese state. That has always been a critical issue in Chinese thinking since ancient times. Modern nationalism has intensified that sentiment for China's communist leaders, especially as the appeal of communist ideology has waned. The nationalist sentiments of the Chinese communists, however, can be a mixed blessing for Hong

Kong. On the one hand, it is associated with a pride in demonstrating that Hong Kong can be run successfully without the British and, on the other hand, it is associated with a fear that Hong Kong and its freedoms may subvert communist rule on the mainland. Matters are not helped by the fact that very few Chinese officials are sufficiently appraised of what makes Hong Kong work as to be able to weigh the delicate balance between these contradictory impulses.

THE ECONOMIC DIMENSION

The economic significance of Hong Kong may be said to be a direct result of the communist victory in China in 1949. For the previous hundred years Hong Kong had been a relative backwater, servicing little more than Guangdong Province as it was outshone by Shanghai. However, the advent of the communists led many of the more entrepreneurial Shanghainese to flee to Hong Kong. While Shanghai atrophied and decayed under the centralist and anti-bourgeois Maoist regime, Hong Kong rapidly began to build itself afresh after the influx of more than two million refugees. The American economic embargo that was imposed on China at the outbreak of the Korean War in June 1950 proved to be a boon in disguise as it forced the colony to develop its own manufacturing industries and move away from its earlier entrepôt role. At the same time it became the principal avenue through which the communist regime earned a modicum of hard currency that was still necessary for its largely autarkic command economy. It was through Hong Kong that remittances were sent by Overseas Chinese to their relatives on the mainland. These were estimated at $500–600 million per year when the total value of trade in the 1960s rarely reached $4000 million. In fact, if the bill for supplying Hong Kong with water and food were added, it would be clear that the huge country of China gained nearly half its hard currency income from the tiny British colony.[4] Moreover, during the Maoist period from 1949 to 1976, Hong Kong was China's principal gateway to the capitalist world. It was there, for example, that the grain deals with Canada, Australia and Argentina were reached initially to alleviate the acute shortages in 1961 that had been caused by the disastrous Great Leap Forward.

As China changed course at the end of 1978 to embrace the policies of economic reform and openness to the international economy, some thought that Hong Kong's significance would decline as China would no longer use it as its main point of access to the capitalist world beyond. But Hong Kong adapted to the new situation to become even more important to the Chinese economy and to its engagement with the international economy. Hong Kong manufacturers were quick to take advantage of the cheaper land and labour force across the border so that by the early 1980s three million of the four million people employed in Hong Kong factories were located across the border in China. This meant that at a stroke the Chinese economy had access to the managerial know-how, the appropriate technology and the marketing skills of Hong Kong so that in one fell swoop the Chinese were able to bridge the gap between their low quality and unfashionable styles of clothing to reach the demanding high standards and latest fashions of western markets. However, Deng Xiaoping and his advisers had from the outset shrewdly recognised what an enormous asset their compatriots in Taiwan, Macao and especially Hong Kong could be. Four Special Economic Zones were opened adjacent to these territories so as to attract their investment and export skills. The most notable of these is Shenzhen, across the border from Hong Kong, which has mushroomed up from being a sleepy village of twenty thousand inhabitants in 1978 to becoming a bustling modern city of two million people within fifteen years.

In 1985, Hong Kong became China's biggest trading partner until it was overtaken by Japan in 1993, but from the outset Hong Kong became and remained its biggest foreign direct investor.[5] Hong Kong has accounted for between 60 and 80 per cent of the total foreign direct investment in China. According to Chinese official statistics, by 1993 there were 50,868 investment projects of Hong Kong and Macao businesses in China with a contract value of $76.754 billion and actual utilisation value of $17.862 billion. The bulk of these were located in Guangdong Province across the border,[6] but as the detailed breakdown of the statistics of the foreign trade and direct foreign investment of each of China's thirty provinces and municipalities showed, Hong Kong ranked either first or second in both categories in all but five of them.[7]

Clearly, the economic impact of Hong Kong on China is immense and can hardly be exaggerated, but by the same token, as Chinese officials are quick to point out, so is the significance of the Chinese economy for Hong Kong. Governor Patten made the following point in 1994 in surveying the decade since the Sino-British Joint Declaration agreed on the future of China:

Trade with China had grown by 500 per cent in real terms so that

China had become the largest market for the territory's exports and the biggest supplier of its imports; China had become the biggest investor in Hong Kong as Hong Kong had become the biggest investor in China. The benefits for Hong Kong had been immense as total GDP grew by 79 per cent in real terms; and the growth of per capita GDP had elevated the ranking of the territory from 28th in 1984 to 17th ten years later. As manufacturing had shifted across the border, Hong Kong had increased its weight as an international business centre with the service sector providing 75 per cent of GDP and 70 per cent of total employment.[8]

The benefits for China cannot be measured in economic statistics alone. The huge growth of the service sector in Hong Kong is indicative of the scale of the service that the territory provides for the mainland. In the absence of a legal culture on the mainland and its shifting regulatory character for the conduct of business, it is hardly surprising that Hong Kong with its internationally respected rule of law and with its reliable and efficient financial services has become the main base for the conduct of business with China. The territory not only provides China with the facility for myriad economic exchanges with the outside world, but it is also a major centre of learning where China's key international trade and investment organisations acquire expertise and invaluable experience in dealing with the many facets of the international economy. Thus, major institutions such as the China International Trust and Investment Corporation (CITIC), China Resources and the Bank of China have been long established in Hong Kong and may be said to understand its economic character well.

Xu Jiatun, the former director of the Hong Kong Branch of the Xinhua News Agency (the official representative of the Chinese government in the territory), once put it well in 1988:

> The principal changes of modern capitalism find expression in the fact that it has a relatively [good] legal structure, which ensures an environment of free competition and which enables the productive forces to develop further.

He concluded that unless legal and operational structures of modern capitalism were mastered, it would not be possible to carry out the socialist modernisation programme properly in China.[9] It might be added that, seven years later, such structures have yet to be mastered in China and that it is Hong Kong which provides a great deal of these services to China. Another measure of the significance of Hong

Kong's role in facilitating China's deepening engagement with the international economy may be seen from the importance of foreign direct investment for China's capacity to export. Although it accounted for less than five per cent of the value of China's output, it was the source for two-thirds of the country's exports.[10] It will be recalled that Hong Kong is responsible for 60–80 per cent of direct foreign investment in China.

In sum, Hong Kong may be said to play crucial economic roles for China, first as perhaps its most important partner in trade and investment and, second, as its most important provider of business services and its key agent in contributing to modernisation. Curiously, Chinese officials are reluctant to acknowledge this publicly. Instead, they prefer to emphasise how dependent Hong Kong is upon the Chinese economy. That may be true, but it is hardly relevant in a context in which China will be re-establishing sovereignty over Hong Kong in a way that could very well damage the institutional basis of its operations precisely because of a failure to understand it.

THE LINK WITH TAIWAN

As seen from Beijing, Hong Kong is intimately linked with Taiwan in at least two ways. First, China's leaders have put forward the same political framework to both places as a basis for re-establishing sovereignty and reunifying the country. Second, Hong Kong is the main economic conduit through which exchanges are conducted with Taiwan.

The concept of 'one country two systems' was first devised with Taiwan in mind. Following the full normalisation of relations with the USA in December 1978, Beijing sought to capitalise on Taiwan's sense of abandonment by its American ally. Putting aside Mao's long established policy of seeking to 'liberate' Taiwan (which implied the overthrow of the nationalist party: the Kuomintang or KMT), Deng and his colleagues proclaimed a new policy favouring peaceful reunification. This ostensibly allowed for the continuation of the capitalist system and KMT rule, but within the sovereignty of the People's Republic of China (PRC). Although the scheme was brusquely rejected by the government in Taipei, Beijing has continued to adhere to it. The ageing communist leaders hoped that they could reach an understanding with the older leaders of the KMT based on old personal ties established in the 1920s and 1930s. The older generation of the KMT was judged to be more attached to the mainland – their place of birth – than the next generation that was born in Taiwan and, in many cases, married to Taiwanese. But the KMT's resistance to the blandishments of the distrusted communists was strengthened by the passing of the Taiwan Relations Act by the US Congress that once again provided a legal framework for an American defence commitment to Taiwan. Once it became clear that there would not be rapid progress in solving the Taiwan problem, Beijing adapted the concept and, with the agreement of the British, applied it to the reversion of Hong Kong to Chinese sovereignty.

As seen from Beijing, if the concept were to work well in the case of Hong Kong, it would strengthen its appeal to the people in Taiwan. Conversely, were it to be seen to have failed in Hong Kong, Beijing would lose the only policy for peacefully reuniting with Taiwan that it has advocated consistently for the last seventeen years since 1978. It would be left with only the military option. The repercussions would be damaging for Beijing: Taiwan would have to strengthen its defences; the USA would be alarmed and may take counter measures; Japan too would be greatly concerned as would be the other countries of East Asia; and China might find that it had put in jeopardy its general strategy of economic engagement with the Asia-Pacific that has been deemed essential for its broader objectives of economic development and modernisation.

Meanwhile, Taiwan has come round to the position of broadly supporting Beijing's policy on Hong Kong. Dropping its initial opposition to the Sino-British Joint Declaration of 1984 as cutting across its own claims to be the true government of China, Taipei in May 1991 formally recognized that China was ruled by two governments and that its own jurisdiction did not extend to Hong Kong. That acknowledged publicly a position that had already developed in practice since cultural and economic ties developed with the mainland via Hong Kong from 1986 onwards.[11] This meant, in effect, that Taiwan was shielded from the full blast of Beijing's attentions until the retrocession to the PRC of sovereignty over Hong Kong was settled in 1997. It also meant that whatever doubts that may be entertained in Taiwan about the feasibility of Beijing to carry out its policy of 'one country two systems' in Hong Kong, Taiwan also had a reason to hope that the policy would not fail.

Interestingly, neither Beijing nor Taipei saw the Hong Kong situation as *fully* analogous to that of Taiwan – although they did so for different reasons. Beijing's view was that as Hong Kong was ruled by Britain, its fate was subject to negotiations between the two sovereign powers without the participation of representatives from the territory. At best, the people of Hong Kong were the putative members of a local Chinese government to be vested with considerable powers of autonomy as worked out between the Chinese authorities and prominent Hong Kong people deemed to be patriotic. Moreover, the future Hong Kong SAR would have to defer to Beijing for defence and foreign affairs. Taiwan being ruled by Chinese could negotiate directly with Beijing either as a prospective local government or as between the Nationalist and Communist Parties. In any event, it would be allowed to retain its own armed forces. The precise terms of what Beijing had to offer would be subject to negotiations, but they would be more generous than what had been offered Hong Kong. Taipei, of course, rejected any analogy at all. Until the late 1980s it had claimed to be the true government of China as a whole and since then it has sought recognition as a separate government altogether.

Nevertheless, both Beijing and Taipei in practice found Hong Kong to be the main conduit for the exchange of visits involving several million people from Taiwan and at least a million from the mainland. It was also the principal place for cultural and even unofficial political exchanges. Above all, it was through Hong Kong that the bulk of the economic exchanges have been conducted.

The economic exchanges between Taiwan and the mainland that have been conducted through Hong Kong have been very important for both sides. The indirect trade in 1993 reached $14.39 billion, heavily balanced in Taiwan's favour as its exports to the mainland came to $12.93. This accounted for 15 per cent of the value of Taiwan's exports, although the total value of trade with the mainland was 8.9 per cent. Taiwanese investment was also important as, by the end of 1993, Taiwan had emerged as second only to Hong Kong in terms of foreign direct investment absorbed in the mainland. There were 21, 193 investment projects altogether with a contract value of $18.95 billion and actual utilisation of $5.1 billion.[12] These economic transactions were important for Taiwan as it enabled manufacturers to stay in business by shifting labour-intensive industries to the mainland and in also enabling its home industries to tap into the growing China market. The economic ties with Taiwan were important for the economic development of the mainland, especially in the two southeastern provinces of Guangdong and Fujian.

The economic ties carried important political messages too. As seen from Beijing, the economic engagement with Taiwan provided significant contacts and networks that were regarded as contributory steps towards unification. In Taipei's perspective, these ties helped to deflect further pressure from Beijing on the reunification issue. The Taipei government also hoped that they helped people in Taiwan to recognise the enormity of the gap between their living conditions and political circumstances and those on the mainland. It was thought that recognition of the wide gulf would strengthen the position of the government on the island, especially as Beijing made it clear that it would oppose by force, if necessary, any attempt to declare the island independent.

Hong Kong, therefore, has played a role not only in facilitating economic and other exchanges between the mainland and Taiwan, but also in contributing to keeping relations between the two sides peaceful. In recognition of this, the Chinese Vice Premier and Foreign Minister, Qian Qichen, issued a seven point guideline for the conduct of exchanges after the resumption of sovereignty in 1997. As to be expected, he argued that relations between Hong Kong and Taiwan will be considered as between two regions of the same country, but the tone and approach was pragmatic as was the response from Taipei. The importance that the two sides attach to the relationship being conducted through Hong Kong can be seen from the fact that Qian's moderate speech was delivered on 22 June 1995 when the airways were thick with Beijing's angry denunciations of Taiwan President Lee Teng-hui's visit to the USA. The Hong Kong link was too important to be damaged by political storms.

HONG KONG AND GREATER CHINA

The term 'Greater China' came into vogue in the late 1980s and early 1990s. It arose to take account of the rapidly growing economic ties between Taiwan, Hong Kong and the two southeastern coastal provinces: Guangdong and Fujian. The economic nexus between them based on the integrating aspects of their respective comparative advantages suggested that a new economic actor was emerging. With Hong Kong at the centre providing entrepôt and international business services and with southern China providing relatively cheap land and labour, manufacturers in both Hong Kong and Taiwan operated a complex triangular network of production and export. Collectively, the three entities accounted for the world's third largest GNP, the largest foreign exchange reserves and third largest trade turnover. Moreover, they ranked in value as the third largest exporter to the USA after Canada and Japan.[13] The highest circles of leaders in Beijing expressed interest in the concept. Deng Xiaoping is said to have remarked that the scheme 'wasn't a bad idea', but warned against discussing the matter in public lest Taiwan suspect Beijing of ulterior purposes and other countries misread it as portending a new 'Yellow Peril'. Jiang Zemin ordered that a high level study be prepared. In early 1992 an international symposium concluded that a process of increased economic cooperation should lead in due course to greater coordination between the different parties, culminating eventually in a new stage of economic integration.[14]

However, the term became controversial and by the mid-1990s it has become less in vogue among Chinese intellectuals in Taiwan and Hong Kong. Part of the reason is that it has acquired separate and conflicting connotations. It can be used to signify the kind of dynamic economic entity sketched above, but it can also be understood to refer to an aggressive China eager to enlarge the area and range of people under its control. Another problem is in delimiting its geographical scope. Several definitions have been identified in terms of ever larger concentric circles most of which centred on Hong Kong. These included: Greater Hong Kong (Hong Kong, Macao and Guangdong); Greater South China (Hong Kong, Macao, Taiwan and the southeastern coast of the PRC stretching as far as Shanghai); Greater *Nanyang* (Hong Kong, Macao, South China, Taiwan, Singapore and the ethnic Chinese entrepreneurs resident in Southeast Asia); All China (Hong Kong, Macao, Taiwan and the entire PRC); and Greater China (Hong Kong, Macao, Taiwan, the PRC, Singapore and overseas Chinese throughout the world).[15]

As a concept, Greater China drew attention to the transnational quality of much of the economic interactions among the various Chinese communities. It further highlighted the disjunction between the informal processes that characterised its operations and the absence of formal institutions to regularise them. In fact, it highlighted the fact that these transnational operations cut across formal boundaries of political entities that were often at odds with each other and whose systems were run on divergent lines. Although this could be presented as the triumph of economics over politics and as yet another piece of evidence to suggest the obsolescence of statehood in face of the global forces of economic processes and technological change, the reality is more complex. The political differences between these entities have precluded the development of institutions to this transnationalism and, to the extent that the various forms of Greater

China are articulated, they run the risk of falling foul to politics. For obvious reasons, all attempts to institutionalise networks of relations involving the ethnic Chinese residents in Southeast Asia risk exposing them to discriminatory reaction by the local states and to hostility from the majority ethnic communities. Perhaps a deeper concern focuses on how a Greater China might be manipulated for political ends by the PRC itself.

After initial enthusiasm, officials and scholars of the PRC began to treat the concept with a degree of circumspection. On the one hand, there would be problems in seeking to unify these different Chinese centres within the framework of the PRC, but on the other, their very diversity could have disintegrative implications for the PRC. Others may have speculated about the desirability of a federal or confederal Chinese state, but the leaders of the PRC still profess the imperatives of a unitary state and, in any case, the PRC still lacks a legal culture necessary for a federal system.

In practice, however, the vagaries and uncertainties of Greater China may be said to work in Hong Kong's favour. Whether defined within the narrower or broader geographical boundaries, the significance of the operations of Greater China lie in its informal aspects. The complex nexus of relations on which the economic ties are based may be said to be those of family, or the long-standing social links between overseas Chinese and their ancestral villages and, more broadly, the networks of relationships defined by complex series of mutual obligations (*guanxi*) that transcend bureaucratic barriers. In other words, the economic links are based less on those of legality and organisational rationality than on the traditional ascriptive ties between groups of people of similar ethnicity and customs that collectively may be called cultural in the anthropological sense.[16] These informal processes that link the disparate Chinese communities centre upon Hong Kong. In the words of that long time observer of Hong Kong and Southeast Asia, Dick Wilson, Hong Kong is 'the capital of the Overseas Chinese'.[17]

These informal links combine to make Hong Kong an asset for the PRC in enabling it to benefit from the manifold associations in general and the economic ones in particular that Hong Kong as the centre of Greater China can provide. Indeed, the more these informal processes are seen to be centred on Hong Kong rather than subject to the manipulations of Beijing, the more successful they can be. In any case, Beijing has its own agenda on Taiwan that would not be satisfied with informal arrangements. As a Deputy Director of the Taiwan Office of the State Council of the PRC noted in August 1992, 'the most important question confronting Taiwan and the mainland was not Greater China, but the normalization of relations'. He added, 'without the acceptance of direct postal, transportation and commercial links across the [Taiwan] Straits, the idea of a Greater China or of a Greater China Commonwealth is nothing'.[18] One of the implications of those observations was that until the Taiwan issue was resolved, Hong Kong would continue to be the linchpin for the operation of the informal economic networks that had proved to be so important for China's economic miracle.

Perhaps the most important reason that has enabled Hong Kong to play this role has been precisely because of its special character of British-inspired freedom under the law. Its openness as a free port where capital and goods can move in and out and where people can come and go and work with very few restrictions has also been important. Moreover, despite the British colonial presence, Hong Kong has been rightly described as a 'very Chinese international city'.[19] In terms of the politics of the region, Hong Kong has been largely neutral. Recognising that its survival has depended upon not being seen to subvert China's fundamental interests, while at the same time being a useful window or even a gateway to the world, Hong Kong has long eschewed playing a part in regional politics. Meanwhile, of course, it has been a highly active member of the international (capitalist) economy. Even as an overtly British colony it has been able to pursue its own independent self-interested path since at least the late 1950s.[20] Thus, it was a congenial meeting point for many of the Chinese Overseas not only because it was often their point of departure from southern China, but because it was not seen as challenging to the various governments in whose countries they resided. Moreover, as Wang Gungwu – the leading historian of the Chinese Overseas – has observed, 'Hong Kong was recognized by all as the pivot for the most effective economic links with China, especially for all non-official relationships through and with South China'.[21]

The Chinese Overseas, especially in Southeast Asia 'where Chinese ethnicity has to remain subdued', seek reassurance that the PRC will be able to sustain the policies that have encouraged the emergence of Greater China. They will look for evidence of a stable regime whose policies are not easily unsettled by the policies of other powers. According to Wang Gungwu, most of the long settled and naturalised ethnic Chinese business people will not have been swayed by the developments so far towards a Greater China, but will have waited for clearer signs of stability in the PRC and of its government's 'capacity to adjust to new global and regional relationships'. The wealthiest among them 'with bases in Hong Kong' have so far limited themselves to 'short term investments made through their Hong Kong bases'. Wang concluded that 'even these entrepreneurial Chinese have balked at being exposed to the uncertainties that still hover around the growth of Greater China'.[22]

The PRC clearly has much to gain by allowing Hong Kong to continue in its present path after 1 July 1997 and, correspondingly, it has much to lose by seeking to bend the territory to its control. Hong Kong's pivotal role in Greater China that has been so beneficial to the PRC would rapidly decay if its current freedoms under an impartial law were seen to have been eroded by the intervention of Beijing or by the seepage from the north of the corruption and bureaucratic practices typical of the business culture there. Similarly, if, following the transfer of sovereignty, Hong Kong's conduct in the international economy were seen to be subordinate to the interests of the PRC, the Chinese Overseas could rapidly disengage. That would damage not only Hong Kong, but the mainland as well.

HONG KONG AND THE POLITICS OF MODERNISATION

Since December 1978 when Deng Xiaoping led the programme of rapid economic development through economic reform and openness, Chinese politics (as recognised within China itself) has oscillated between a reformist tendency to loosen (*fang*) administrative and ideological controls and a conservative tendency to tighten them (*shou*).[23] These tendencies may be seen to reflect deeper structural divisions in the Chinese economy as it lurches towards modernity in the uncharted way of 'crossing the river by feeling for the stones on the river bed'. On the one side is the state sector epitomised by the state-owned enterprises and, on the other, the collective, private and foreign-related sector. At the onset of the reforms, the state-owned enterprises accounted for ninety-five per cent of the value of industrial production, but fifteen years later by the end of 1993 (according to official figures that undoubtedly inflated their true contribution to the economy), they accounted for less than fifty per cent. Indeed, although they consumed sixty per cent of all fixed-asset investment in China, their share of gross industrial output fell from two-thirds in

1985 to little more than two-fifths ten years later in 1995.[24] The relationship between the two sectors is highly complex and it involves interdependencies as well as competition. The distinction between the two sectors is the degree to which they are subject to direct administrative controls rather than one of strict ownership in legal terms, as the collective and private sectors are largely run by officials or former officials. However, the distinction is nonetheless important. There can be no doubt that the trend favours the non-state-owned sector and that is the sector that is most closely associated with Hong Kong. But the state centric sector is deeply embedded within the main institutions of the state and, as a result, the Hong Kong factor gets drawn into the politics between the two tendencies.

Another way of thinking about the two tendencies is by reference to the famous television series *River Elegy* (*He Shang*) that was shown in 1988. The series greatly angered the Party elders. Using the image of the stagnant meandering Yellow River, it stigmatised Chinese history as isolationist, xenophobic and resistant to change. It depicted a common chauvinistic dogmatism to the Confucianism of the feudal period and to the Maoism of the contemporary period. It was only once these brown stagnant waters reached the crystal blue waters of the ocean that salvation became possible in the shape of modern (western) technology, institutions and values.[25] Drawing on these images it is possible to describe the conservative state centric tendency as epitomising the deep seated continentalist tradition in Chinese history and depict its adherents as the 'Browns'. The adherents of the reformist tendency which is oriented to the modernity emanating from the maritime direction may be depicted as the 'Blues'.[26] The 'Browns' of course generally correspond to those normally described as conservative and the 'Blues' to those regarded as reformers or radical reformers. In these terms, Hong Kong is clearly associated with the 'Blues'. To appreciate the significance of this in current Chinese politics, the issue must be put in the appropriate historical context.

In the annals of Chinese nationalism, Hong Kong symbolises the first instance of a long list of shameful and humiliating acts that were to demean and even threaten the extinction of the Chinese state during the hundred years after it had been ceded to Britain by the first unequal treaty of 1842. The retrocession of sovereignty in 1997 is accordingly of deep significance, but the cession of Hong Kong in 1842 arose out of China's defeat by the more modern naval forces of Britain. Accordingly, it has another significance in Chinese history as the first and disastrous encounter with the modern industrial world. Thereafter, Chinese history may be depicted as a series of attempts to come to terms with modern (sometimes equated with the 'Western') world of industrialism, trade, continually advancing technology and its corollaries of social change and new forms of statehood.

Indeed, nationalism and quest for modernity went hand in hand. The purpose of modernisation was often seen by the leaders of the state and their advisers to preserve what they regarded as authentic Chinese values. These were generally seen as antithetical to the western or capitalist values associated with modernity itself. Consequently, modernity has tended to be seen in instrumental terms as a means to acquire sufficient wealth and power to resist encroachments upon the Chinese State and subversion of its social values. Ultimately, modernisation was seen as the means to restore China to its rightful place at the centre of world affairs. However, no modern Chinese leader envisages that long-term goal being achieved before well into the twenty-first century at the earliest. Meanwhile, the more defensive instrumental approach prevails.

Thus, at the heart of the thinking behind Deng Xiaoping's economic reform programme is a problem that troubled the nineteenth-century reformers who sought to modernise along Western lines while retaining Chinese traditional Confucian values. Deng's goal of embracing foreign capitalist practices in order to develop 'socialism with Chinese characteristics' is reminiscent of the goals of the Confucian reformers of more than a hundred years ago. Their slogan was 'Chinese learning for the essentials and Western learning for the practicalities' (*Zhong xue wei ti, Xi xue wei yong*). That encapsulated the reasons for their failure, as Western technology and managerial know-how were subversive of Confucian values.[27] The same may yet be true of the current attempt as applied to Chinese Communist values. There are parallels, for example, between the resistance of the more old-fashioned upholders of traditional Confucianism in the nineteenth century to what they regarded as disruptive Western intrusions and the resistance of old-fashioned upholders of traditional Communism in the current period to alleged western subversion.

The parallel with the past should not be drawn too sharply as there are many important differences. However, much though it may have been adapted to Chinese conditions, Communism itself is ultimately derived from the West. More importantly, China is no longer closed as it once was. There are many social forces and groups who have been heavily permeated by Western influences. As the Tiananmen events showed, China is part of the 'global village'.[28] The position of the Chinese Communist Party, the nominal upholder of orthodoxy that might be thought to epitomise the approach of the 'Browns', is highly complex as many of its members at all levels are actively engaged in what might be called entrepreneurial activities more appropriate to the 'Blues'. Perhaps an even more important difference from the situation of the Confucian reformers of the nineteenth century is that the 'secrets' of modernity are possessed not only by the dreaded Westerners, but by fellow Chinese on the once despised maritime periphery. As we have seen, this is particularly true of the compatriots of Hong Kong who are due to return to the embrace of the motherland.

What has been depicted here as a struggle between the 'Browns' and the 'Blues' must be understood in a wider context. China is experiencing a fundamental shift in its centre of gravity from being focused on an age-old continentalist orientation to one that is acquiring more maritime orientation. The continentalist orientation is deeply rooted in Chinese history with its preoccupation in administering an essentially agrarian economy and protecting the state from nomadic enemies from the heartlands of inner Asia to the north and west. It is a tradition associated with the upholding of civilisation through a unitary bureaucratic state. The civilisation and the institutions associated with it crumbled before the Western onslaught in the 'century of shame and humiliation' to be replaced after immense upheavals by the communist regime in 1949 amid claims that the 'Chinese people had stood up' and had established a 'New China'.

In terms of continentalism the 'new' China had much in common with the 'old' and even exceeded it in some respects. Its orientation was inwards; its strategy was concerned with continental military defence; its economy was subject to tight state administration; and its bureaucracy was subject to a totalist ideology that was guarded zealously against alien infusions. Since the onset of the economic reforms under the leadership of Deng Xiaoping, this continentalism has been shaken by the roots. The orientation is outwards in the sense that the sources for economic reform no longer come from the Communist Party or the Marxist canons of political economy, but are derived from the private sector and, more particularly, from capitalist external influences beyond the sea shores. China's military strategy has been refocused towards the development of rapid reaction forces and to acquiring naval capabilities better able to uphold the country's newly developed maritime interests. The most productive and successful sectors of the economy have been precisely those that have not been directly administered by the state and which have a maritime orientation or coastal location. Although some of the very large state-owned enterprises have been economically successful and even an important source of revenue for the national budget, it is the state-owned sector as a whole that is in crisis and that is holding back the country from developing a legal rule-based regulatory structure appropriate for a more market-run economy. Meanwhile, communist ideology, which had already lost its grip on the younger generations by the end of the Cultural Revolution, decayed in the face of the opening to the West and the erosion of the Communist Party's controls over people's lives.[29]

The Party's continued grip on power depends upon its being able to preside over a rapidly growing economy that ensures rising prosperity for most people. This leads to something of a paradox as the only way in which continued economic growth can be assured is through deepening the engagement with the capitalist world beyond the sea shores. This entails the admission of influences that are subversive to communist rule – what Deng has called the 'flies and insects' that come in through the open door. The counter to these influences is the Party's emphasis on the virtues of stability. The emphasis on stability is appealing to many who still vividly remember the chaos and disruptions of the Maoist years culminating in the ten-year Cultural Revolution. The attraction of stability is reinforced by the vision of the troubles that have assailed the Russian people since the demise of the Soviet Union and its communist party.

The shift towards an ever greater maritime orientation may seem inevitable from a long-term historical point of view, if only because of the need for continued economic growth to meet the needs of its vast and growing population. But it is no easy matter to transform the traditions and the deeply ingrained patterns of thought accumulated over thousands of years to meet immediate utilitarian needs. More-over, in the short term (with which we are primarily concerned) there are immense problems to be addressed and vested interests to be encountered. The problem of the state-owned enterprises may be taken as but one example to show how some of the differences in addressing some of the more intractable domestic problems may impact upon the treatment of Hong Kong for good or for ill.

The evolution of the state-owned enterprises (SOEs) is central to the concerns of the 'Browns'. These remnants from the Soviet socialist past employ more than 100 million people – the bulk of the urban work force. In the past, their role extended beyond the economic to be units of social welfare and organisation for their employees who were attached to them for life. Not surprisingly, most of them are highly inefficient by the criteria of the capitalist market. However, they represent the core of what is left of the socialist sector, they also account for most of China's heavy industry and they provide most of the country's power, transport facilities, defence industries etc. As the administered part of the economy they are well represented in the central ministries and bureaucracies in Beijing. Among the many problems that they represent arising out of their manifold inefficiencies is that, according to official figures, half operate at vast losses and all of them are caught up in what are called triangular debts in which they owe each other enormous sums for produce and supplies. Despite the relative success of some, the SOEs have become a huge black hole absorbing an ever-growing proportion of the state budget. All are agreed that reform is necessary and all agree that a short sharp shock that would throw the worst offenders into bankruptcy is not feasible since it would be socially too destabilising to create a huge army of unemployed and of unpaid pensioners.

At this point, opinion is divided. The 'Blues' favour subjecting the SOEs to the rigours of reform to meet market forces, albeit on a graduated basis, for their ultimate aim is to move the country towards a macroeconomic system appropriate to a market economy and away from administrative controls. The 'Browns', being loathe to surrender administrative controls and still inspired by the traditional vision of the paternalistic state that exercises ultimate responsibility for the welfare of its people, take a different approach. In their view, the SOEs represent the core of the socialist market economy and they have suffered from unfair competition from foreign-related enterprises in particular. What is required, therefore, is to exercise better controls over foreign investment and target it towards major infrastructure projects in conjunction with the SOEs. In 1994 such views were linked to attempts by the centre to reassert its power by 'socialist interventionism' and by developing an industrial policy.[30] The difficulty in attaching names to these different tendencies may be gauged from the fact individual leaders may change their positions. For example, Zhu Rongji, one of the members of the Standing Committee of the Politburo, has generally advocated allocating more weight to market forces, but in 1994 he shifted to a more statist position on this issue.[31]

As far as Hong Kong is concerned, it has a benign and positive role to play in the vision of the 'Blues', but as seen by the 'Browns', Hong Kong is more of a problem whose investments and influences need to be brought under more central administrative control. Given the oscillations in Chinese politics between loosening (*fang*) and tightening (*shou*) that are linked to the economic cycles of boom and retrenchment, much will depend on what point is reached in the cycle around the time of the reversion of sovereignty in 1997.

On 1 July 1995 the Chinese government published four major documents that together amounted to its most comprehensive policy statement on its priorities regarding inward foreign investment. These, on the whole, favoured the interests of the SOEs. They also sought to encourage investments that introduced high-technology and advanced management and that were directed towards the interior, as opposed to investments in labour-intensive enterprises and those directed towards the coastal provinces. The policy also clarified that any investment valued at above $30 million required the prior agreement of the central government. Broadly speaking, these documents favoured the agenda of the 'Browns'. They appeared in the course of the build-up to the Ninth Five Year Plan when the perspectives of the 'Browns' were in the ascendent. Moreover, they were published at a time when the retrenchment policies were still being applied. It should be recalled that the previous Five Year Plan (1991–1995) which had called for a measured growth of 6–8 per cent a year was set aside as a result of the personal initiative of Deng Xiaoping whose speeches on his 'southern tour' of early 1992 mobilised support to prevail over the more cautious planners in Beijing with the result that the annual growth rate for the five years averaged 11.7 per cent. In the absence of a strong man, it is possible that the relatively slower rate of 8–9 per cent projected for the 1996–2000 Five Year Plan may prevail, but it is highly unlikely that the central authorities will be able to change the balance between the coastal and interior provinces. In 1984 they accounted for fifty per cent of China's GDP. Ten years later after the GDP had more than doubled, the coastal share rose to fifty-seven per cent and most economists expect that trend to continue. In the same period, Shanghai's distinction as the leading source of China's exports was easily eclipsed by Guangdong Province which, by 1994, accounted for forty per cent of the value of the country's exports. The significance of Hong Kong may be further attested by the fact that, despite having shifted more than two-thirds of its manufacturing capacity to the mainland, the value in 1994 of its own exports (i.e. excluding re-exports) came to about $30 billion as compared to the total of $120 billion for the whole of China.[32]

Hong Kong has continuously demonstrated a significance for the Chinese economy and for the modernisation of the country that would be difficult to exaggerate. Yet it has done so without formal arrangements with the Chinese authorities. Since Hong Kong has been perceived in the PRC as neither a foreign nor a domestic issue there is no major bureaucracy at the heart of the government or state structures that takes responsibility for the management of its affairs. That means that there is no institutionalised route through which Hong Kong matters can be brought to the attention of senior leaders and key economic bureaucracies. The organisations charged with managing the transition towards the reversion of sovereignty do not have the requisite high standing and, in any case, their brief does not extend to the broader issues of the territory's place in China's overall economic development. Even though nearly all the major economic organisations in China are represented in Hong Kong in one way or another and some of them, such as CITIC and the Bank of China, understand Hong Kong well and play important roles in linking it with the economy of the mainland, there is no evidence to suggest that they actively bring Hong Kong issues forward in the determination of the major economic decisions in Beijing. Hong Kong's influence is therefore felt indirectly by its sheer economic weight and by the informal networks of ties that bind it to southern China in particular. Hong Kong may be seen as a major factor, if not a direct player, in the complex politics of modernisation. However, once sovereignty has been regained, Hong Kong could play an even more crucial role in the modernisation of the country, especially as its chief executive would then have a direct line of communication to the State Council and its premier.

HONG KONG AS AN INTERNATIONAL ENTITY

By virtue of its current colonial identity and its future role as an autonomous region of China, Hong Kong does not enjoy the constitutional independence necessary for recognition as a state, but it has nearly all the attributes of statehood. Despite its small size of about 1000 square kilometres, it has a population of six million and a well developed bureaucratic and administrative system allied to the effective rule of law. It is virtually self-governing in its own domestic affairs. Indeed, if domestic criteria were to be applied, Hong Kong is better qualified to act as a state than a majority of those recognised as such in the United Nations. Although Hong Kong is not responsible for its defence and foreign relations, the scope and importance of its external relations is very large and of international significance.

Its peculiar status is recognised internationally. The governments of about ninety states are represented by consular or trade missions and a number of sub-national governments (provinces, states etc.) also maintain representative offices in the territory. Since these are nominally accredited to the UK, Hong Kong is not required to reciprocate. But Hong Kong probably hosts more foreign diplomatic offices than most states in the world.[33] By an act of Congress in 1992, the USA is required to treat Hong Kong as 'a non-sovereign entity distinct from China for the purposes of domestic law based on the principles of the 1984 Sino-British Joint Declaration'. The act further states that the USA should 'continue to fulfil its obligations to Hong Kong under international agreements as long as Hong Kong reciprocates, regardless of whether the People's Republic of China is a party to the particular international agreement'. It added that Hong Kong should continue to be treated 'as a separate territory in economic and trade matters'. Canada had passed an act a year earlier which also gave special consideration to Hong Kong. An expert in international relations in Hong Kong observed: 'Compared with other autonomous entities, Hong Kong's formal authority to conduct its external economic and cultural relations and to take part in international organisations is therefore unparalleled'.[34]

Because of its special political position, the activities of the Hong Kong government in international affairs have been confined primarily to economic matters. Its external representatives, for example, have largely left aside international political and security issues, and have confined themselves largely to trade negotiations and trade and industrial promotion. Hong Kong, however, did follow the British position in severing economic links with Argentina during the Falklands War and in 1986 it imposed import restrictions on South African goods in line with British policy. Perhaps the most notable example of Hong Kong's engagement in international politics was the lobbying of the American government between 1989 and 1994 in favour of the renewal of the granting of Most Favoured Nation to China. Hong Kong's own economic interests were directly involved, but it showed that the growing connection between politics and economics may yet draw Hong Kong into a more active role in the overlapping areas between the two.[35]

There is another sense in which Hong Kong's peculiar position in international politics has been of great significance, especially to China. Namely, during the Cold War period that facilitated its role as a gateway to the international capitalist economy. Since then, Hong Kong has been the gateway for countries that did not at first recognise the PRC, notably South Korea, but especially Taiwan. Moreover, the absence of sovereignty has enabled Hong Kong to take advantage of its status to cultivate the more informal aspects of international relationships as indicated earlier in the discussion about Greater China and the various links with the Chinese Overseas in Southeast Asia. At the same time, Hong Kong is a member or associate member of many international and regional organisations, including the Asia Development Bank, the General Agreement on Tariffs and Trade (GATT) and its successor the World Trade Organisation, the UN Economic and Social Commission for Asia and the Pacific, the Asia Pacific Economic Cooperation forum (APEC), Interpol and many others. In fact, membership of thirty such organisations has been agreed by the Sino-British Joint Liaison Group (JLG).

However, the main significance of Hong Kong's international identity springs from its economic prowess. Tiny Hong Kong is the world's eighth largest trader, it ranks fourth as an international banking centre and it holds the sixth largest amount of foreign trade reserves. In 1987 it passed Rotterdam to become the world's largest container port. The territory is the most important centre that combines finance, communications and transport in the Asia-Pacific. It is also the key link between the Chinese economy and the rest of the world. There can be little doubt that as an international entity, Hong Kong contributes greatly to the economic development of China.

In conclusion, it should be pointed out that other aspects of Hong Kong's significance to China such as those involving culture and foreign relations beyond the transition will be discussed in subsequent chapters. But it is clear from those dimensions touched on in this chapter that Hong Kong is of enormous significance to China even in its present form under a British-led administration. Providing that the transfer of sovereignty were to be handled with care, the contribution of Hong Kong could be greater still.

Chapter 2

Differences between the Hong Kong and Chinese systems

One of the important requirements for the successful operation of the concept of 'one country two systems' is that each 'system' should have a good working knowledge of the other. In other words, it is not only desirable, but highly necessary, that each side should appreciate those aspects of the 'way of life' (to quote the distinctive but ambiguous phrase of the Joint Declaration) of the other that will facilitate orderly relations. Given the disparities in size and power between mainland China and tiny Hong Kong, it may be thought that the only important question is the extent to which the Hong Kong 'system' is understood by the appropriate persons and institutions on the mainland. That may indeed be the primary question, but it is also vitally important that those in Hong Kong who will have to manage relations with the 'system' on the mainland will understand how to operate effectively within it.

As we have seen, the mainland and Hong Kong have interacted with each other in important ways since the establishment of the communist government in 1949. Nevertheless, despite the inter-dependent quality of those relations, the two societies evolved amid deepening ignorance of important aspects of each other's 'way of life'. Xu Jiatun, the former Director of the Hong Kong Branch of the Xinhua News Agency, pinpointed one result of this when, complaining about his communist colleagues back in China, he explained in 1988: 'They always judge capitalism by old standards. They do not notice its changes. Had I not worked in Hong Kong for four years, I would probably have entertained the same idea as those comrades'.[1] Even senior journalists and officials who have lived in Hong Kong for all or most of their lives who work for communist newspapers and organisations complain privately that their colleagues from the mainland have 'a totally different mentality' that causes them to misunderstand 'even simple things' about Hong Kong.[2]

In Hong Kong, too, there was ignorance of the way the mainland worked. The civil service in Hong Kong operated until very recently without contact with or knowledge of administrators and officials on the mainland. One example of a serious misunderstanding to which this gave rise concerned the question in 1994 of passing onto the Chinese authorities information about senior civil servants so that, in due course, they could make informed judgements about appointments to senior positions. The Secretary for the Civil Service refused to hand over the personal files in which tests of the suitability of the person including matters of private life style were included. In fact, a senior member of the department told me that such materials were routinely destroyed after the appropriate interviews had taken place. The Chinese side promptly objected that important material information was being deliberately withheld. Neither side knew or understood the practices of the other. In China, personnel dossiers are the key to all appointments and are integral to the Party-state system and it would be inconceivable to remove anything, especially of a compromising nature, from them.[3]

Dealings with China were handled by the Office of the Political Adviser to the Governor – which was in effect a branch of the Foreign Office in London. Hong Kong basically worked in the shadow of China, but without direct formal contact with it. It was only after it had been formally agreed in 1984 that sovereignty would revert to China in 1997 that a fuller range of contacts and exchanges began to develop between the mainland and Hong Kong. Curiously, it could be argued that the best period of relations with the PRC over Hong Kong occurred during the period of indirect contact, or coexistence, before 1984 when there was no need to reconcile their fundamental differences.

COEXISTENCE 1949–1984

Britain and China

Hong Kong depended for its existence on a series of tacit understandings between Britain and China, Britain and the people of Hong Kong, and between the people of Hong Kong and China. The first of these between Britain and China were the most important as the other two hinged upon it. It was also the most remarkable. Hong Kong had an anomalous existence as a British Crown colony perched on the underside of the PRC which was one of the staunchest opponents of imperialism and colonialism in both its domestic and foreign policies in the world. The anomaly was made possible by the compatibility of their two apparently contradictory understandings of the position of Hong Kong. In the British view, Hong Kong was legally a colony by virtue of the three treaties of 1842, 1860 and 1898. The first two had ceded in perpetuity the island of Hong Kong and Kowloon respectively, and the third had leased the 'New Territories' up to the Shenzhen (Sham Chun in Cantonese) River and associated islands for ninety-nine years until 1997. As seen from Beijing, the three treaties were invalid as they were 'unequal'. Hong Kong was therefore Chinese territory that was being administered by the British until such time as the Chinese people should decide to take it back. Meanwhile, it was implied if the British chose to base their rule on those treaties, it was in principle their affair and it did not imply any acceptance of the validity of those treaties by the Chinese side.

The divergent interpretation of the legal basis for British rule meant that it would not have been possible to reach formal agreements. The ways by which understandings were reached had by necessity to be based on adjustments to the initiatives of the other as buttressed by informal arrangements. The anomalous situation worked because both sides, and especially the Chinese side, saw it in their interests that it should work. As with all such arrangements, much depended on the initial steps.

The reasons as to why the victorious communist army stopped at the Hong Kong border of the Shenzhen River in October 1949 will remain a matter of speculation until all the evidence becomes available from the Chinese archives. Meanwhile, evidence from Soviet archives suggests that as early as January 1949 (three months before the crossing of the Yangtze River) Mao Zedong had already decided to defer the seizure of the two remaining western colonies of Hong Kong and Macao because of their economic value to China as bases for foreign trade.[4] But it is likely that Mao also saw Hong Kong as a possible venue through which to develop relations with the West once he had eradicated all traces of the Western presence in China and was able to establish diplomatic relations on a basis of what he regarded as genuine equality. He called the policy, 'inviting guests after cleaning the house'. The ever-suspicious Stalin thought that Mao aimed to establish relations with Washington and he was much troubled by the British decision to recognise the new China that was announced on

6 January 1950 (the day after Truman had declared that the USA would not intervene to prevent a communist takeover of Taiwan). Accordingly, Stalin pressed Mao to seize Hong Kong, but the latter refused. On the other hand, Mao accepted the Soviet proposal to denounce the legitimacy of the representative of Nationalist China at the United Nations which also included the Soviet offer to support China by boycotting the Security Council.[5] The immediate effect of this was to make it more difficult for China to deal with America since the latter was not quite ready to abandon altogether the Nationalist regime on Taiwan.[6]

This shows that, from the outset, the Hong Kong issue was considered a very important question by none other than Mao. He saw it as having a crucial role to play in the conduct of China's foreign trade and, perhaps more importantly, in the management of China's foreign relations with the West. Its significance can be seen by the fact that he turned down a request that he seize it from no less a person than the mighty Stalin on whom Mao depended if he were to gain an offer of protection from the USA and the military assistance necessary for an attack upon Taiwan. Both of these were vital if the revolutionary victory were to be safeguarded and the civil war completed. It is possible that Mao and his military commanders were deterred by the British reinforcement of Hong Kong which the British Foreign Secretary, Ernest Bevin, described as 'the Berlin of the Middle [*sic*] East'.[7] It is more likely, however, that Mao and his colleagues had already determined to leave Hong Kong in British hands, but at first they were constrained from exploiting it for foreign policy purposes other than trade because of the suspicions of Stalin and because of their preparations for the attack on Taiwan.

Meanwhile, practical matters such as trade across the border were handled on an *ad hoc* basis. The Xinhua News Agency Hong Kong Branch which had operated since 1945 as something more than a news agency became in 1949 the *de facto* representative of the PRC government and its ruling communist party. This suited both the British and the Chinese sides admirably, as a formal consulate would have been an embarrassment to both of them. The Chinese, however, pressed unsuccessfully for the appointment of a commissioner.[8] The British feared that a Chinese commissioner or a consulate would become an alternative source of authority. China's leaders too probably came to appreciate the value of informal arrangements. This allowed them greater flexibility and the absence of formal representation did not affect China's overwhelming local superiority in military terms. Moreover, this way the Chinese avoided any embarrassment as being perceived to have conceded a degree of legal recognition for British rule in Hong Kong. Henceforth, the News Agency and the Office of the Political Adviser to the governor became the main channel for the conduct of local official business. As mentioned earlier, the latter in effect represented the Foreign Office in London. This was acceptable to the Chinese side as it conformed to their view of Hong Kong as being a Chinese place under temporary British administration. The people of Hong Kong were regarded officially as compatriots and representatives from them were selected to sit on the national representative bodies in Beijing. By dealing directly with the representative of the British Foreign Office the Chinese were able to avoid any complications that may have arisen from dealing with local representatives.

Hong Kong's position was, in fact, settled by the outbreak of the Korean War. The War fixed Sino-American relations in a state of enmity that was to last more than twenty years; it led to American protection for Taiwan; and it caused the USA to impose an economic embargo upon China. The latter forced Hong Kong to end its entrepôt role for China and to transform itself into a base for manufacture. Nevertheless, Hong Kong still imported its food from the mainland and arrangements were soon made to import water as well. Hong Kong then became, bit by bit, the main foreign currency earner for Beijing.

In the early 1950s Beijing saw no need to expel the British. In addition to its economic role, Hong Kong was the main point from which Beijing gained access to the Chinese Overseas in Southeast Asia. Beijing also did not wish to antagonise the British as they were seen to be a restraining influence on the Americans.[9] For Britain, too, Hong Kong was still of strategic importance in view of its commitment to the emergency in Malaya against the largely Chinese communist insurgency. The main trouble for British colonial rule in Hong Kong stemmed from activities by anti-communist Nationalists and occasionally their American backers.[10] By 1957, however, with Malayan independence established and the end of the 'emergency' in sight, British strategic interests in the Far East were rapidly dwindling. The Hong Kong garrison was reduced to levels appropriate for the maintenance of internal security only, and in 1958 the naval dockyard was closed. As far as Britain was concerned, 'from that date Hong Kong was an appendage, one without any strategic significance, and from which decreasing commercial advantage was to be expected'.[11]

However, the British reached a secret agreement with the USA in 1957 that in return for not pressing for the admission of the PRC into the United Nations, the USA agreed to regard Hong Kong as 'a joint defence problem'.[12] By this stage, the British had also begun to pay more heed to Beijing's interests in restraining Nationalist activity. Discrete attention was also paid to the international concerns of the PRC by keeping away representatives of the Soviet Union and its East European allies. When the Chinese Foreign Minister protested in 1965 about the use of Hong Kong by US forces engaged in the war in Vietnam, a shift of arrangements was made to meet his concerns.[13] Interestingly, when the violence of the Cultural Revolution spilled over into Hong Kong, US servicemen were not made targets for attack even though on occasions they were present in tens of thousands.

The final element in the Sino-British understanding about Hong Kong was that there would be no movement towards democracy or self-government. That would have been seen by Beijing as preparatory for independence which was clearly unacceptable. By this stage, it had long been recognised by Britain that colonial rule in Hong Kong was only possible with the consent of Beijing. Leaving aside its strategic vulnerability, Hong Kong depended on the mainland for food, water and effective policing of the border to prevent floods of refugees that would otherwise swamp the place.[14] As the British Minister of State, Judith Hart, explained in February 1967:

> Hong Kong is in a completely different position from any of our other Colonies. For international reasons alone, there are problems in planning for the usual orderly progress towards self-government. Because of Hong Kong's particular relationship with China, it would not be possible to think of the normal self-government and not possible, therefore, to consider an elected Legislative Council.[15]

Not even the riots of the summer of 1967 that were occasioned by the spill-over of the Cultural Revolution changed the fundamentals. As soon as Zhou Enlai regained control a little later that summer, the *status quo ante* was restored. Indeed, it was perhaps strengthened as a result of having been put to the test.

In 1971, Zhou Enlai told Malcolm MacDonald (the former Commissioner-General for Southeast Asia) that China would not seek to recover Hong Kong until the expiry of the New Territories' lease in 1997.[16] Matters were clarified still further following the Sino-

American rapprochement as expressed in the Shanghai communiqué of 28 February 1972. This raised doubts about the remaining significance of the 1957 American commitment to the defence of Hong Kong. Five days later, the Chinese representative on the Security Council had Hong Kong and Macao removed from the list of colonial territories named by the UN Committee on Decolonization on the grounds that they were part of Chinese territory occupied by Britain and Portugal arising from the unequal treaties, and that the settlement of the questions 'is entirely within China's sovereign right and does not fall under the ordinary category of "Colonial Territories" covered by the declaration on the granting of independence to colonial countries and people...'. The British did not put forward an alternative view. A week later on 13 March, a joint Anglo-Chinese communiqué was issued raising their recognition to full ambassadorial status. Edward Heath, who as Prime Minister had negotiated the new relations with China and who enjoyed good relations with their leaders, visited Hong Kong as leader of the opposition in 1974 and confirmed that it would be handed back to China in 1997.[17]

The terms by which Hong Kong was to be run until the handover was negotiated had now been clarified. In short, they embodied the two basic points for the informal arrangements that had applied since 1949 – a Chinese tolerance for British rule in return for British acceptance that there would be no self-rule, with the implication that Hong Kong would return to Chinese sovereignty at some future date, probably 1997. But at the same time, China's shadow had been drawn in sharper outline and, as if in recognition of this, official documents of the (British) Hong Kong government dropped the word 'Colonial' from the titles of chief secretaries and even stopped calling the place a colony, referring to it instead as a 'territory'.

Britain and the people of Hong Kong

Here, too, there was a tacit understanding that might have been called a kind of a social contract. The role of Britain, or rather the (British) Hong Kong government, was to keep the communists out, provide clean government in return for which the people were expected not to challenge the authority of the government.

Interestingly, in 1946 the Governor, Sir Mark Young, reflecting the ethos of the Colonial Office under the new Labour government in Britain proposed to introduce a measure of democracy in Hong Kong. At the time, Britain was resisting the claims of the Nationalist government that was backed by the USA. The suggestion was eventually shelved in 1952 by the less enthusiastic Governor, Sir Alexander Grantham (who had succeeded Young in 1947). In part, this was because of difficulties in identifying an appropriate elect-orate. The last available census of British subjects had been taken in 1931 and showed a total of 73, 866. In 1945 the total population was put at 600, 000 and by March 1950 it had been swelled by refugees to reach an estimated 2.3 million. By the summer of 1952 before a modified plan which had already been agreed by the British Cabinet was made public, the Governor was persuaded by a delegation of the leading members of the Executive and Legislative Councils 'to stop this madness which will be the ruination of Hong Kong'. They maintained that there was 'no real demand whatever' for extended representation, which had been foisted on them by 'a doctrinaire Colonial Office'.[18]

In the event, no public demands for participatory democracy followed. Nor were there demands for the end of colonial rule.

> There was a complete absence of political agitation of any sort and the population showed a clear preference for continued British rule rather than subjection to Communist control.[19]

Indeed, as many have observed, for the period from the end of the Second World War until the early 1980s, the vast majority of the Chinese population had no interest in the business of government and showed no desire to participate in political activity. The bulk of the population in the early 1950s were made up of refugees who had fled the civil war and the communist forces in particular. Although little was done to house the tens of thousands who lived in appalling conditions in squatters camps until the mid 1950s, the only three serious incidents of rioting that led to deaths that took place were primarily inspired by the peculiarities of the politics of the National-ists and the communists. In addition to these there were about twenty incidents of confrontations between police and demonstrators that involved minor injuries, and these arose from industrial disputes or from resistance by squatters to compulsory clearances of their huts.[20] Meanwhile, considerable economic changes had taken place. By the 1960s, Hong Kong had been transformed from an impover-ished colony swamped by refugees into what was officially described as 'a stable and increasingly affluent society comparable with the developed world in every way'.[21]

When asked, the population tended to identify itself as 'Chinese' rather than as Hong Kongers. The bulk of these people were migrants from Guangdong Province where they still had relations and where their ancestral village was located. There was also an enormous social and cultural distance between the bulk of the population and the British élite. Yet these largely displaced people, nevertheless, gave their support to the (British) Hong Kong government when it was challenged by riotous Nationalists in 1956 and even when confronted by the more serious challenge of the Cultural Revolutionaries in 1967.

The British government in London largely left the Hong Kong government to its own devices. That government tended to confine its activities in the 1950s and 1960s to what has been described as a select set of 'essential' functions revolving largely around law and order and the provision of the basic social and urban services required by a capitalist economy.[22] As in other colonies, the government was headed by a governor appointed from London who in principle possessed awesome powers. He was advised by an Executive and a Legislative Council made up of senior officials and local notables, including some of the leading Chinese entrepreneurs. Government administration was and continues to be relatively centralised. In the 1950s and 1960s when the role of government was fairly circumscribed, the numbers of people employed in the public service was relatively small. Thus, in 1952 and 1962 they came to 22, 900 and 48, 277, respectively.[23] By the 1990s their numbers had expanded to around 200, 000.

A major change took place in the 1970s. The government responded to the improved economic and social circumstances by upgrading expenditure on housing and infrastructure, but more importantly, the character of the Hong Kong population began to change as the children of the refugees of the early 1950s came to maturity. Unlike their parents, they knew no other place and regarded Hong Kong as their permanent home. They tended to be better educated than their parents and they had been taught within an educational system whose curriculum had been heavily influenced by Britain. Also, having been brought up in a cosmopolitan city open to a vast array of international influences and having benefited from the freedom of the press, radio and television, they were less constrained than their parents by traditional Confucian influences or by the experiences of the civil war and the upheavals of revolutionary China. By the late 1970s many of these were beginning to constitute a new middle class of professional people. A survey of public opinion conducted in 1977 revealed that fifty per cent of those interviewed favoured having elected members in the Legislative Council. Among those with a post-secondary education, the figure was seventy-one per cent.[24] It was around this time that embryonic political groups began to emerge in the territory.[25] The Hong Kong government in the 1970s responded to these social changes by increasing its processes of consultation and encouraging the development of interest groups.[26]

In sum, the British provided an efficient administration, an effective legal system and an infrastructure appropriate to a free port practising *laissez-faire* capitalism. The Chinese people of Hong Kong were able to enjoy all the fruits of a free society except for self-rule, but at no stage did they, like most other colonial subjects, agitate for self-rule. The shadow of China made them appreciate the benefits of what they had and it reminded them of what might lie in store for them if they were to threaten to undermine the terms of Chinese tolerance for the continued separate existence of Hong Kong. This did not mean that the majority of the population positively enjoyed being ruled by foreigners – British rule was accepted. In most other respects, Hong Kong was very much a Chinese city (albeit an international one) and in a poll taken two years before the Joint Declaration of 1984, more than sixty per cent of Hong Kong's residents identified themselves as 'Chinese'. Only a third called themselves Hong Kongers and a quarter admitted to roots in Britain. In 1988, less than a third identified themselves as 'Chinese' and nearly two thirds professed a strong sense of belonging to Hong Kong.[27] The difference between the two polls reflects the concern after 1984 to demarcate Hong Kong and its way of life from that of the mainland to whose sovereignty it would soon revert.

China and the people of Hong Kong

As we have seen, Beijing consistently regarded Hong Kong as a part of China that was administered by Britain until such time as the Chinese government and people deemed it appropriate to reclaim it. The people of Hong Kong, like those of Taiwan, were designated as 'compatriots' (*tongbao*). This distinguished them from the Chinese Overseas who were regarded either as Overseas Chinese (*huaqiao*, technically, Chinese citizens resident overseas) or as people of Chinese ethnicity (*huayi* or *huaji*). The generic name for all kinds of Chinese is *huaren*. Provision was made for Hong Kong representation in the Chinese People's Political Consultative Conference (CPPCC) which had been set up in 1946 as an umbrella body for all the political parties in China. By 1949, the CPPCC had come under the control of the communist party and it was used as the first representative organisation of the People's Republic. When the National People's Congress was established in 1954, delegates from Hong Kong were also selected to attend and the CPPCC reverted to becoming the principal united front organisation.

Thus, under the terms set by Beijing, the Hong Kong people had multiple identities. They were 'compatriots' who were formally represented on the main representative bodies of the state even though they were under temporary British administration with whom they were supposed to cooperate. More than half of their number held British passports and, until the British changed their nationality laws in 1961 and 1971, they all could claim the right to reside in Britain. They were also members of the united front organisation of the PRC and the CCP, both in the class sense as members of the national bourgeoisie, the working class etc., and in their capacity as a bridge to the *huaqiao* and *huaji* in Southeast Asia especially.

No special bureaucracy was established in Beijing to deal with Hong Kong or the compatriots living there. It was a matter in which Mao, occasionally, and Zhou Enlai, continuously, took an interest. Practical matters were handled through the Xinhua News Agency Hong Kong Branch which represented both the PRC and the CCP. Monetary remittances from locals and from Chinese communities in Southeast Asia to relatives in southern China were handled by the Bank of China branch in Hong Kong. Since Hong Kong was said to be a part of China, it was regarded as belonging to Guangdong Province and, accordingly, a special section of the provincial government was set aside to cover Hong Kong, but it was never clear as to what its precise duties were. In fact, from the perspective of Beijing, Hong Kong did not fit into any clear category for bureaucratic purposes as it did not fall into the purview of either foreign or domestic affairs. Moreover, unlike Taiwan whose people were also regarded as compatriots, it did not raise high political questions associated with the civil war or strategic questions associated with the USA and problems of separatism.

There were people close to the senior leadership in Beijing such as Liao Chengzhi and members of Zhou Enlai's entourage who had intimate experience of living and working in Hong Kong both before and after the Japanese occupation. Some of these also had good working relations with some of the established leading business families among the Chinese Overseas in Southeast Asia. The personal ties that these well-connected people enjoyed with senior figures among the established leading business families in Hong Kong served Beijing well, especially in the 1950s and 1960s. However, as they suffered in the course of the class struggle movements at home, especially during the Cultural Revolution that lasted for ten years, the nature of the contacts weakened. Moreover, their Hong Kong interlocutors, not surprisingly, came to value their separate Hong Kong identity more highly.

The main problem with these personal and essentially informal linkages was that they did not extend to the new generation either in the PRC or in Hong Kong. So that as the PRC emerged out of the Cultural Revolution in 1976, few in the younger generation had any experience, knowledge or understanding of the outside 'bourgeois' world of the West, let alone of such a complex place as Hong Kong. Meanwhile, the older generation of 'experts' in matters concerning the Chinese Overseas and Hong Kong were simply out of touch with the new middle class that had emerged in prosperous Hong Kong. Thus, Beijing became increasingly out of touch with the more modern developments in Hong Kong. This led to a contradiction by which the PRC government welcomed the economic advantages that the modernity of Hong Kong had to offer, while being suspicious of the society and culture that had given rise to it. In the eyes of the more conservative (or leftist) communists, Hong Kong was a dangerous source of 'spiritual pollution'. It was easier to blame the decay in public morality and the rise of corruption in the PRC on an external agency, such as Hong Kong, than to confront the implications of their having arisen because of deep flaws within the domestic system. However, such sentiments and the ignorance about Hong Kong and the way that it worked were suggestive of a huge gap in understanding that had developed in Beijing's approach to the people of Hong Kong.

As we have seen, for their part too, hardly any of the people in Hong Kong had a good understanding of the way the PRC worked. One Hong Konger who took the trouble to go and work in China for a year in 1983 said that when he first arrived,

I could not understand its people's attitude or thinking, even though we were both Chinese. *I felt a complete foreigner.* Yet after only a year, I appreciated their point of view and, whether I agreed with them or not, I at least understood them.[28]

(Emphasis added)

There had always been a groundswell of patriotic feeling on which Beijing might have expected to draw, but its own egregious behaviour tended to militate against that. In other words, by the late 1970s and early 1980s, the weakest link in the arrangements underpinning the coexistence between the PRC, Britain and Hong Kong was that between the Chinese (*Huaren*) on both sides of the Shenzhen river.

THE CULTURAL DIFFERENCES AFTER 1984

The signing of the Sino-British Joint Declaration in 1984 made it even more necessary that Beijing should forge a network of relations with the people of Hong Kong. Only thus could a smooth transition of sovereignty in 1997 be assured and only on that basis would it be possible to operate successfully the 'one country two systems' thereafter for the next fifty years or more. However, the experience of the (more than) ten years since then suggests a mixed result at best.

Since 1984, the Chinese authorities have made some attempts to bridge the gap, but these cannot be rated a great success overall. The great problem has been the impact of the Tiananmen incident of 4 June 1989 when the horror of seeing live on television tanks and soldiers on the streets of Beijing killing hundreds or more of peaceful demonstrators sent shock waves through the territory. A million people (or twenty per cent of the total population) marched through the centre of Hong Kong in protest. The head of the Xinhua News Agency, Xu Jiatun, who had been brought in 1983 and who had made a great impression in reaching out to different groups and shades of opinion removed himself to America in 1990. His replacement, Zhou Nan, restored tight discipline to the much disturbed Xinhua Branch, but at the same time alienated many by his hardline 'leftist' approach. In the view of the leaders in Beijing, Hong Kong, which had been heralded as a major economic asset up to that point, began to be seen in 1989 as a dangerous subversive influence.

Curiously, in view of its importance, Hong Kong has been relatively neglected as an object of study by China's universities and research institutes. The long-standing bureaucratic problem of being unable to locate it as an issue of either foreign or domestic affairs still remains. There is an institute attached to Zhongshan University in Canton (Guangzhou) which touches on the issue, but that focuses mainly on economics. Other than that, there are researchers attached to Xinhua in Hong Kong and to the Hong Kong and Macao Affairs Office in Beijing who give advice on policy, and the occasional researcher (usually of junior status) attached to institutes of European studies. In the course of five visits to China since 1990 dealing with the country's premier universities and research institutes, I have been unable to find researchers working on politics and society in Hong Kong despite repeated requests to meet them.

At the same time, there is hardly an organisation of note in China that is not represented in Hong Kong in one form or another. Similarly, the families of China's most prominent leaders are active in the territory. Their interest, of course, is in making money. It is possible that in the process of doing so they have developed a deeper understanding of how Hong Kong works and of its complex society. If so, there is precious little evidence to that effect that is publicly available. There are, in fact, important Chinese organisations who are very knowledgeable about the territory and its economy, but so far they have carefully refrained from becoming involved in the politics of Sino-Hong Kong relations. These include institutions such as the Bank of China, China Resources, the China International Trust and Investment Corporation and many others.

There are signs that the senior leaders in Beijing are aware that something is seriously amiss in their understanding of Hong Kong. In a talk in March 1995, that was understandably very well received in Hong Kong, Li Ruihuan, a member of the Standing Committee of the Politburo of the CCP, publicly admitted that the leaders had a dangerously insufficient understanding of Hong Kong. He warned that 'taking Hong Kong back is an unusually complicated job' with 'many issues and difficulties' and that 'it is inevitable that we shall fail to manage some things appropriately and well'. He went on famously to compare Hong Kong to a hundred-year-old Yixing tea pot whose value lay in some sediments attached to the inside. This was destroyed, however, by the act of cleaning it by a well-meaning, but ignorant old lady so that the prospective purchaser lost interest. Li drove home his message by concluding,

> if you don't understand something, you are unaware of what makes it valuable and it will be difficult to keep it intact.[29]

Meanwhile, the popular culture of Hong Kong has spread far and wide in China. It appeals in particular to the young, many of whom have abandoned the public collectivist values of the older generations in favour of finding identity and meaning in the more personal worlds associated with popular music in particular.[30] That, too, has not translated into a better understanding of Hong Kong and its people.

The appeal of the popular music of Hong Kong (and also that of Taiwan) has to be understood in terms of the receptive audience in the mainland, but it does point out the lack of appeal of the officially approved culture for the masses. It also illustrates the gulf of understanding between the mainland's world of officialdom and the commercialised popular culture of Hong Kong itself.[31]

The Joint Declaration in 1984 came at a time when the distinctiveness of the social and cultural systems associated with the emergence of the middle class in the late 1970s had become evident. The public statement that the two sovereign powers had agreed formally that the territory should revert to Chinese sovereignty had a galvanising effect that gave a political edge to these social changes. This was felt most strongly because, during the transition period, both sides had apparently committed themselves to introducing a significant element of democracy so that Hong Kong people would be able to exercise a high degree of autonomy after the transfer in 1997.

New political groups were formed and some went on to become political parties. In 1985 the first limited elections to the Legislative Council took place as a few seats for functional constituencies were made available.[32] However, much of the initial enthusiasm was curtailed as it became apparent that Beijing had a rather restrictive approach to democracy in mind and that the British and Hong Kong governments intended to converge with the Chinese approach.

The Chinese authorities have traditionally enjoyed good lines of communication with two kinds of groups in Hong Kong, who are not necessarily best placed to advise on matters involving the concerns of the burgeoning middle class and professional people, that form the backbone for the operation of much of the modern economy of Hong Kong. These groups are: the local Chinese entrepreneurs and, second, perhaps up to ten per cent of the labour force which, since the 1940s, has been affiliated to pro-Beijing trade unions and whose children attend pro-Beijing schools.[33] The entrepreneurs tend to dominate their businesses personally in association with their families. Their business practices are those of traditional Chinese Overseas entrepreneurs where reliance is placed on personal trust and personal networks (*guanxi*). That may be contrasted with most large international business corporations where management is more bureaucratic and rule-based and where business practice relies heavily upon the rule of law. They have consistently been unsympathetic to democratic tendencies fearing the development of ever greater demands for welfarism. The danger is that Beijing may regard those who have been 'friends' for many years as fully representative of 'capitalism' in Hong Kong. In any event, Beijing has yet to demonstrate that it has good lines of communication with the broader strands of the professional middle class.

Much more is now known about the social structure and political attitudes of people in Hong Kong because of the more systematic surveys by social scientists that were stimulated by the 1984 announcement about the reversion of sovereignty to China in 1997. Among other matters, such surveys have facilitated a clear delineation of the socio-political dimensions in which Hong Kong differs from China. These have been listed as follows:

1 There is in Hong Kong more social and interpersonal trust, personal freedom, civil liberty and social and political tolerance.
2 There is more tolerance of social conflict, less fatalism and less egalitarianism.
3 Economics are distinguished from politics and are accepted as being non-egalitarian, the capitalist system being fully endorsed.
4 Hong Kongers expect fair treatment from government and are less frightened by it.
5 Law is respected and distinguished from politics.[34]

It will be recognised that these attributes of Hong Kongers are those normally associated with a democratic society and they embody essentially middle-class values. Leaving aside the question of the degree of democracy that Beijing may finally allow the post-1997 SAR, it is these attributes which most Hong Kongers fear are not fully recognised and understood in Beijing.

Hong Kong is also a bustling international city with a door that has been open to goods, ideas and people. It has a lively expatriate population of nearly a quarter of million people. Its Chinese population of 5.8 million comprises different groups from southern China, many of whom have family ties in Southeast Asia and some have family ties in Western countries including, more recently, the Western countries of the Asia-Pacific. Its population is highly mobile. At the time of the 1991 census, 151, 833 of its 5.5 million residents were temporarily away from Hong Kong – or three absentees per hundred. But at the time of the lunar New Year, up to a million – or a fifth – of the population will be absent. In 1992 more than 77 million people passed through Hong Kong as tourists or en route to and from China. In short, unlike any Chinese city on the mainland or perhaps anywhere else, Hong Kong is that seeming contradiction: a Chinese cosmopolitan city. It is also the most important centre for the dissemination of information and news in Asia and a major regional base for many of the world's media giants. It is at the forefront of information technology.[35]

There are other distinctive social qualities possessed in the territory that are perhaps best captured by Hugh Baker's categorisation of 'Hong Kong Man'. He or she was described as neither Chinese nor British. This person was

> quick-thinking, flexible, tough for survival, excitement-craving, sophisticated in material tastes, and self-made in a strenuously competitive world. He operated in the context of a most uncertain future, control over which was in the hands of others, and for this as well as for historical reasons lived 'life in the short term'.[36]

One response of 'Hong Kong Man' to the new uncertainties created by the agreement to hand the territory back to China in 1997 has been to leave. Or rather, to establish a right of residence abroad. According to the official Hong Kong year books, more than 500, 000 have done so in the eleven years since the Joint Declaration of 1984. The main target countries for emigration have been Canada, the USA, Australia and New Zealand. As a result, these countries have developed new social and economic relations with Hong Kong that have given each a deeper interest and stake in the other.[37] A common pattern that has emerged is for the mother and children to be established abroad while the father returned to work in Hong Kong. The official estimate is that 'at least 12 per cent of those who emigrated in the 10 years before 1994 have returned'.[38] The fast-paced working environment of Hong Kong was familiar, the skills of the father were appreciated and money could be made more quickly.

In addition to the professionals who have foreign passports, or at any rate who have a right of residence abroad, most of the Hong Kong business people are also in the same position. Even many of those who describe themselves as 'pro-Beijing' have retained the option to leave. The conventional wisdom is that up to 500, 000 could exercise a right to reside abroad immediately, but a senior government official claimed privately in August 1995 that the figure was as high as one million. There is little doubt that most of these people would prefer to stay and prosper in Hong Kong. Moreover, many would also prefer to bring back their families lest their children should lose their Chinese cultural identities in the educational and social milieu of the West. Their decision will depend on how Beijing manages the transfer of sovereignty and how it treats Hong Kong thereafter. This provides Beijing with an opportunity as well as a danger. But what is required is for it to acquire a better appreciation of Hong Kong society than it appears to possess.

Broadening the awareness in Beijing of Hong Kong society is not just a question of widening the means of communication between the two sides. From the perspectives of Beijing, Hong Kong is not just a tiny place that is useful to the economic development of China. Behind it looms the history of humiliation by Western (in this case, British) imperialism with whom the final account is due to be made. It also symbolises the forces of modernity and capitalism. It is also a part of the southern (Cantonese) maritime periphery. These elicit ambivalent reactions and evoke different responses from different groups within China. For the more traditionally-minded (conservative or 'leftist') communists, Hong Kong is more of a problem than an opportunity. Its culture and what it represents threaten an already damaged and decaying communist ideology that cannot be disavowed without undermining still further the legitimacy of the communist party itself. Hong Kong's economic influence in China is seen by these conservative communists as, at best, a mixed blessing as they hold it responsible for contributing to the problems of the state-owned enterprises and to the spread of corruption. They also regard Hong Kong as a destabilising factor in intensifying the regionalisation of the country, especially in the south.[39] Such views also find institutional support in many of the central ministries and in the Propaganda Department of the CCP. Even the more modernising tendencies would not necessarily be free of all these sentiments. Crossing the cultural divides between the mainland and Hong Kong will clearly pose immense difficulties for the leaders in Beijing.

Chapter 3

The troubled negotiations[1]

Once it was recognised that the ending of the lease on more than ninety per cent of the territory meant that China would resume sovereignty, both the British and Chinese sides accepted that it would be necessary to reach an agreement in order to avoid undermining Hong Kong. A way had to be found to meet their different approaches to meeting the common objective of enabling Hong Kong and its people to continue to prosper in a stable way in accordance with the way of life that had allowed the territory to flourish. Despite this common objective, the differences between the British and Chinese have continually made the negotiations a difficult and trying exercise for all concerned. In particular, the British have never wholly succeeded in persuading the Chinese side that the territory's great economic success stems from the rule of law and civic freedoms that underpin its capitalist practices. For their part, the Chinese have always distrusted the British and, perhaps more seriously, have failed to win the hearts and minds of the people of Hong Kong.

The representatives of China and Britain have been negotiating the reversion of the sovereignty of Hong Kong in one form or another more or less continuously since 1979. Despite having reached agreement about the future of Hong Kong in the Joint Declaration of 1984, and not withstanding subsequent agreements that were also proclaimed by both sides as highly satisfactory, the negotiations themselves have been marked all along by distrust. This was aggravated by the Tiananmen incident of 4 June 1989 which caused the British to attempt to restore the confidence of people in Hong Kong against their future sovereign while, at the same time, it alerted China's leaders to what they regarded as the danger of political subversion from Hong Kong. Perhaps the most important indication of the deepening discord in Sino-British relations was the failure to agree upon the method for the September 1995 election of the Legislative Council. The former British Cabinet Minister, Chris Patten, who was appointed Governor in 1992 had aroused the anger of the Chinese government by both the substance and the manner of presentation of his proposals for electoral reform. After vehement denunciations of Governor Patten for allegedly violating earlier agreements, the Chinese side then undertook to replace it with a provisional Legislative Council upon the reversion of sovereignty.

The Chinese have long suspected a British design to abscond with the surplus capital of Hong Kong and to leave the territory in disarray in the hands of an influential pro-British group. Indeed, in the aftermath of the Tiananmen events of 1989 and the collapse of communism in Eastern Europe and the Soviet Union, China's leaders believed that the British were in league with others, notably the USA, in seeking to subvert communist rule in their country. These dark suspicions then became subsumed in their rejection of Governor Patten's proposals for democratic reforms of 1992 and it was not until 1995 that the Chinese agreed to cooperate with the British. This occurred at a time when China's relations with the USA began to deteriorate sharply and it indicated that Beijing no longer thought that London was in league with Washington. Yet the other reasons for distrust remained. For their part, the British have perceived the Chinese leaders as ill-informed and brutal in their exercise of power, and their negotiators have at times been likened privately to street fighters.

The reasons for the distrust are deeply embedded in the cultural differences between the two sides. China's leaders are heirs to a civilisation with a continual tradition of statehood that traces itself uniquely back to ancient times. They are imbued with the nationalist reaction of hurt pride because of the 'century of shame and humiliation' inflicted primarily by the western powers. Moreover, as communists they share the Leninist and Stalinist senses of being in perpetual struggle with the capitalist world.[2] The British, by contrast, being heirs to the very different European civilisation and traditions of statehood with a democratic political culture, have necessarily seen the world in different terms.[3]

The original conflict that had led the Chinese to cede Hong Kong in 1842 arose from the cultural and ideological gulf between the two sides, although it was occasioned by the Chinese attempt to stop the trade in opium conducted under British protection. But one essential difference 140 years later, when the Hong Kong issue once again became subject to formal negotiations with Britain, was that the power relations had reversed. Britain had long ceased to be a significant force in Asia, whereas China had become a major regional power with global influence. Although it was in China's interests to arrive at an agreed settlement, there was never any question that this time it was the Chinese who held the whip hand. In retrospect, it is evident that it was China's undoubted capacity to have reclaimed Hong Kong at any time of its choosing that allowed the territory to continue to be administered by the British for so long. As we have seen, that was made possible because the relevant understandings between Britain and China were tacit and implicit. The latent problems and differences emerged only once British and Chinese representatives addressed the Hong Kong issue formally and directly.

Several problems arose in the course of the negotiations that bear upon the distrust that has made Sino-British cooperation so difficult despite their common interest in effecting a smooth transfer of sovereignty. These include the problems of mutual understandings and misperceptions; and the difficulties of structuring the negotiations in the transitional period.

A BRIEF REVIEW OF THE HISTORY OF THE NEGOTIATIONS

The first step to alter the tacit understandings that had prevailed hitherto was taken by the British side. The advent of a new leadership in Beijing committed to economic development and eager to enhance its economic links with Hong Kong provided the opportunity. The expiry of the New Territory's lease on 30 June 1997 provided the impetus to explore matters with the Chinese, as the remaining eight per cent of Hong Kong's land area which had been ceded in perpetuity had become so integrated with the rest that it was not viable by itself. The British side claimed that the immediate problem was to satisfy accountants, insurers and the like about extending commercial leases beyond the 1997 deadline. The option of altering the terms of the head-lease unilaterally was rejected, lest that provoke a hostile reaction from the Chinese even though they did not recognise the legal standing of the treaty. If the Chinese were to agree about extending the commercial leases, it was hoped that they might accept the continuation of British administration after the reversion of sovereignty to China.

Thus, the then Governor, now Lord MacLehose, raised the issue with Deng Xiaoping when he visited Beijing in March 1979. But it was Deng who first referred to Hong Kong. Presumably, he knew that in 1971 Zhou Enlai had told the senior British diplomat Malcolm MacDonald that China would not seek to recover the territory before 1997, and he would surely have recalled having told the former Prime Minister, Edward Heath, in 1974 of his government's intention to take it back in 1997.[4] With that in mind, the broad terms of what he proposed to MacLehose would have seemed quite generous from a Chinese point of view. Deng explained that China had consistently claimed sovereignty over the territory, but it recognised its special status. There were 18 years left and discussions could be held before then. Whatever the political solution, investment would not be affected. He compared it to Taiwan where he said the return to Chinese sovereignty would not change the social system or the living standards there. Hong Kong would also be a special case. China needed Hong Kong, and a flexible policy, such as he had outlined, would help socialist construction. In response to MacLehose's proposal on the commercial leases, Deng simply reiterated his main point that the capitalist system would continue in Hong Kong for many years ahead alongside the socialist system in China. China had not decided when it would resume sovereignty, but it would continue to 'recognize current realities'. It was not clear whether Deng had understood that MacLehose had not referred to the main so-called head-lease, and subsequent attempts by British officials to clarify the proposal were rebuffed by the Chinese side. MacLehose returned to Hong Kong to say that Deng provided reassurances by telling investors that they should 'put their hearts at ease'. He did not say, however, that Deng had made it clear that he also intended to regain sovereignty.[5]

Taiwan was the greater priority for Beijing. In the autumn of 1977, one of China's most senior leaders told a visitor from Hong Kong that Mao had once said, 'as far as Hong Kong is concerned, we will worry about it after we have liberated Taiwan'.[6] However, by the end of 1981 it had become clear that despite fleshing out the details of their proposals on Taiwan, China's leaders had made little progress. They blamed this upon the intransigence of the leaders in Taiwan whose weakened position at being 'abandoned' by President Carter had been stiffened by the advent of President Reagan. The Chinese accordingly turned to the Hong Kong issue.

The Chinese and British sides prepared their negotiating positions and began the actual negotiations in 1982 'with the common aim of maintaining the stability and prosperity of Hong Kong'. The British side initially argued for the retention of British administration as the surest way of doing so, but it effectively gave way after the Chinese side showed in September 1983 that, where the issue of sovereignty was involved, it was prepared to risk the collapse of the Hong Kong economy and when a deadline was issued after which the Chinese threatened to resolve the issue unilaterally. The British concession gave way to intensive negotiations which resulted in the initialling of the Joint Declaration in September 1984.

By the terms of the Joint Declaration, Hong Kong would revert to Chinese sovereignty on 1 July 1997 as a Special Administrative Region exercising a high degree of autonomy and democracy which would enable it to preserve its existing way of life amid prosperity and stability for the next fifty years. Much of this was spelt out in considerable detail. During the intervening period of thirteen years, Britain would continue to exercise sole responsibility for the administration of the territory. The Chinese side would meanwhile prepare a Basic Law (or mini-constitution) that would embody the general and detailed provisions spelt out in the Joint Declaration. The two governments committed themselves to effect a 'smooth transfer of government in 1997'. At the last minute, the Chinese proposed that a joint commission might oversee the detailed implementation of the agreement, but the British objected that such a commission would undermine the authority of the government and, instead, it was agreed on a British recommendation that a Joint Liaison Group be established to help implement the agreement. On British insistence it was specifically excluded from being an organ of power. On Chinese insistence a separate Land Commission was established to monitor land sales and the equal distribution of premium income between the British Hong Kong Government and that of the post-1997 one. The two sides also agreed to cooperate in the implementation of the agreement to preserve Hong Kong's economic prosperity and its social stability and the JLG would intensify its cooperation in the second half of the transition period. The Joint Declaration, which is regarded by both sides as an international treaty, has since served as the framework for the evolution of Hong Kong.

Thereafter, the implementation of the Joint Declaration involved increasing the democratic basis of the Legislative Council amid close consultations with the Chinese side; the negotiating of agreements in the JLG on issues involving the territory's future international economic arrangements – notable among which were several air services agreements and Hong Kong's accession to the General Agreement on Tariffs and Trade ; the Pacific Economic Cooperation Council (PECC) and the forum for Asia Pacific Economic Cooperation – and more domestic matters such as the localisation of a wide range of laws etc. The British and Hong Kong governments were subject to considerable criticism in both London and Hong Kong for being unduly sensitive to Chinese pressure to restrict the pace and extent of the introduction of further democracy into Hong Kong.

Beginning in 1986, the Chinese side prepared for introducing the Basic Law. A drafting committee of fifty-nine members was established of whom twenty-three were from Hong Kong and this was assisted by a Consultative Committee of 180 members. A first draft was published in 1988 and a second one in February 1989. The prevailing constitution of Hong Kong was colonial and authoritarian in tone, even though in practice many of its executive powers were little used, or applied in a relatively tolerant fashion that might not be true when applied later under the authority of the Chinese Communist Party. In the absence of the democratic institutions in Hong Kong they had to be negotiated into the Basic Law. But conversely, since the British were committed to 'mirror-imaging' the Basic Law, democratic change in the sense of introducing direct elections could not be introduced before 1991 as would be stipulated by the Basic Law.[7] Indeed, by 1988 it was professed that British policy was to seek convergence with the Chinese proposals for the SAR in the hope that a 'through train' would conduct Hong Kong smoothly from British to Chinese sovereignty in 1997. It was under these terms that an exchange of letters took place between the British and Chinese foreign ministers in January and February 1990 about amending the Basic Law before it was enacted by the National People's Congress in April 1990.

By this stage, however, the events of Tiananmen had soured relations and damaged confidence within Hong Kong. Britain was one of the Western countries that applied sanctions and it also postponed the next scheduled meeting of the JLG. Despite his professed desire for convergence, Governor Wilson, in keeping with the feelings of the people in the territory, condemned the Beijing killings and sought to re-establish confidence in the territory in several ways including encouraging London to extend the right of abode to significantly more Hong Kong British passport holders, by introducing a bill of rights, and by developing the huge new airport project that had already been recognised as necessary for Hong

Kong's long-term viability. The Chinese side was angered by these developments as it claimed that its actions in Tiananmen were a necessary reaction against counter-revolutionaries aided and abetted by external forces, some of whom were to be found in Hong Kong. In particular, Beijing singled out the Hong Kong Alliance for the Support of Democracy in China whose leading lights were the prominent liberals Martin Lee and Szeto Wah. It promptly strengthened the clause in the Basic Law against subversion. Although all the British schemes to enhance confidence were denounced by the Chinese side, most, such as the bill of rights and the offer of passports to 50, 000 heads of households deemed important to the viability of the territory, could be carried out unilaterally. The big exception was the airport project. The need for a new airport was not in dispute, but the project was put forward at this time in order to attract foreign investment and thus demonstrate that there was international business confidence in the future of the territory. The trouble was that such investment would need to have the approval of the Chinese side before banks would be prepared to provide the necessary finance. It was this need for their approval that gave the Chinese authorities their opportunity to demand and obtain ever greater consultation over the scheme in particular and Hong Kong affairs in general.

The airport issue was seemingly resolved in September 1991 when Prime Minister John Major went to Beijing to sign the Memorandum of Understanding as agreed during the secret visit of Sir Percy Cradock a month earlier. The Chinese Premier, Li Peng, had used the issue to bring over his British equivalent as the first West European leader to visit Beijing since Tiananmen. According to Cradock, Major's visit went well, and he negotiated an agreement about the formation of Hong Kong's Final Court of Appeal that was due to replace the Privy Council in London. Major nevertheless determined to change the Governor in accordance with a British custom of entrusting an experienced political figure with the management of the last period of the transfer of colonial authority – as had been the case in Rhodesia/Zimbabwe, where the task fell to Lord Soames. That had also been the intention of Mrs Thatcher.[8] The choice fell upon Chris Patten as a result of the fortuitous loss of his parliamentary seat despite having played a critical role in bringing about the victory of the Conservative Party in his role as its chairman.

By then, the first direct elections had been held in 1991 to the Legislative Council. Twelve of the eighteen seats were won by candidates of the United Democrats headed by Martin Lee and another three by independents sympathetic to their point of view. None of the candidates sympathetic to Beijing won a seat, although they were represented in the twenty-one functional seats. Of the remainder, three were *ex officio* and eighteen appointed by the Governor. The new Legislative Council promptly rejected the bill that would have set up the Court of Final Appeal as it allowed for only one foreign judge.

In his first address to the Legislative Council in October 1992, the new Governor proposed a series of political reforms whose combined effect would have greatly extended the franchise for the 1995 elections. He claimed that his proposals did not contravene the Basic Law and he intended to consult with the Chinese following the publication of the proposals. Whatever merit such a procedure may have possessed in the diplomatic practices between West European states, it was a departure from the previous practice of consultation with the Chinese side. Hitherto, the British went public with their proposals only after eliciting Chinese approval following a secret process of negotiation. The Chinese were outraged by both the substance and the way in which the proposals had been advanced and they launched a highly personal series of attacks upon the Governor calling him *inter alia* a prostitute and a snake in language reminiscent of Cultural Revolution Diplomacy. They threatened to establish 'a second stove' or alternative centre of power. Between April and November 1993 seventeen rounds of negotiations were held between the two sides that ended in failure despite a number of concessions by the British. In July that year as a move towards establishing 'a second stove', the Chinese Foreign Minister, Qian Qichen, formally inaugurated a 57-member Preliminary Working committee for the Hong Kong SAR Preparatory Committee (due to be established in early 1996). In December, important elements of the original Patten proposals were voted into law by the Legislative Council, leading to a formal notification by the Chinese side of the intention to dismantle the representative institutions in 1997 and replace them with others in accordance with the Basic Law.

The impact of this was weakened as, within twenty-four hours of the passing into law of the final package of the Patten proposals on 30 June 1994, Britain and China announced they had reached agreement about the disposal of Military Lands. The impression of mixed signals was continued, as on the same day the electronic signboard ticking off the seconds, minutes, hours and days to the reversion of sovereignty was unveiled in the heart of Beijing. In September 1994, the National

People's Congress (the highest constitutional authority in the PRC) unanimously resolved 'to abolish the political structure based on Governor Chris Patten's electoral package'. Yet China's local representatives openly supported the relevant electoral campaigns of sympathetic candidates. Additionally, in September Britain and China finally agreed about the costs of financing the airport. By the summer of 1995 agreements were reached about the major outstanding issues including the Court of Final Appeal (which this time was approved by the Legislative Council) and the authorisation to raise funds for the construction of outstanding developments of the airport. The British trade minister, Michael Heseltine, was warmly received in Beijing in April and the Chief Secretary of Hong Kong (second only to the Governor) Mrs Anson Chan visited Beijing where she was received by senior officials.

This still left important matters to be agreed such as further air services agreements, the rights of abode, the localisation of laws etc. But with less than two years to go before 1 July 1997, the two sides had found ways to cooperate despite the impasse on constitutional matters. Moreover, Beijing had been careful in making its pledges about replacing the representative institutions established under the Patten reforms. It has left its options open as to how much continuity would be allowed in practice between the existing elected bodies and their nominal replacements in 1997. In principle the new bodies could be made up entirely of the representatives of their predecessors, or by completely new people, or indeed by any mix of the two that Beijing saw fit. In other words, the larger process of the Sino-British negotiations will not be completed before the actual retrocession of sovereignty, but it is too early to determine how successful it has been even after sixteen years of more or less continual negotiations.

PROBLEMS OF MISUNDERSTANDINGS AND MISPERCEPTIONS

Sir Percy Cradock who was first posted to China in 1962 and who, from 1979 until his retirement in 1992, was the leading negotiator on the British side, later reflected on 'the longer vistas' of Sino-British relations:

> It is clear that the inevitable contradictions of cultures and political systems have been exacerbated by the fact that both sides have

enjoyed at best partial vision. To us they were the inscrutable Chinese; to them we were the unfathomable barbarians.[9]

The Chinese communists and their advisers appear to have experienced considerable difficulties in understanding the foreign policy perspectives of other countries, especially those of the West and the processes that shape them.[10] Such difficulties that China's cultural legacy may have bequeathed in appreciating and understanding other cultures have been augmented by the additional imprint of the Maoist-Leninist approach. The latter has tended to emphasise an adversarial course in international diplomacy especially in relation to capitalist countries. These have tended to be understood as engaged in attempts to undermine the communist system either by direct confrontation or through cunning conspiracies. In the words of Deng Xiaoping after the Tiananmen incident, the 'western countries are staging a third world war without gunsmoke. By that I mean they want to bring about the peaceful evolution of socialist countries towards capitalism'.[11] China's communist leaders have tended to understand the world in the harsh realist terms of Hobbes and Machiavelli. Regarding Britain in particular the following observations seem apposite:

1 As the oldest surviving imperialist power, Britain is credited with considerable cunning and acumen. In popular folklore, Britain is depicted as a two-headed snake. China's leaders regard it as having managed its relative decline fairly well. Although Suez was regarded as a blunder, Mao Zedong's comment at the time is highly instructive of underlying attitudes:

> The British bourgeoisie, past masters of machination and manoeuvre, are a class which knows best when to compromise. But this time they bungled and let the Middle East fall into the hands of the Americans. What a colossal mistake! Can one find many such mistakes in the history of the British bourgeoisie?[12]

2 Deng Xiaoping, who was born in 1904 and who lived in France from December 1920 to August 1926 where he became a Communist, belonged to that generation of Chinese who witnessed the imperial strength of the British and whose experience of the miseries of capitalist France would not have indicated that the rulers of capitalist Europe were inculcated with a sense of benevolence at home or with altruism in their treatment of Asians under their colonial rule. Not surprisingly, Deng has refused to accept

that the British government is genuinely concerned for the welfare of the people of Hong Kong and that its main interest is in leaving the territory in good order with its people able to exercise autonomy so that the last major act of decolonisation can be carried out with honour and dignity. Britain's leading negotiator later explained:

> As the Chinese saw it, we were in Hong Kong to exploit the territory and extract revenue from it. The British government exercised control over British businessmen there and manipulated the local currency for political ends, as, for example, in the financial crisis of September 1983. The negotiation would be a struggle in which the British as colonialists would prove both obstinate and devious. Deng warned against their tricks. In the end, British commercial and financial interests would need to be satisfied; on this point they were prepared to talk. Our assurances that we sought only the well-being of the people of Hong Kong and recognized a moral responsibility for them were found both baffling and hypocritical.[13]

The early encounters with Britain over Hong Kong brought the distrust to the surface and accentuated it. Chinese officials made it clear that they thought that the British had behaved improperly by bringing up the issue of the commercial leases of Hong Kong with Deng Xiaoping during the MacLehose visit in March 1979 before discussing it with them first. Additionally, it was thought that there was something improper in raising what was regarded as an excessively legalist point in this way.[14] Additionally, having pressed the Chinese in vain to focus on the Hong Kong issue, the British seemed deliberately obtuse in responding to the Chinese approach when it was presented to them in January 1982. Humphrey Atkins, the junior minister with responsibility for Hong Kong, visited Beijing at that point to prepare the protocol arrangements for Mrs Thatcher's Prime Ministerial visit later that year. He saw not only a senior Chinese minister, but he was also received by Prime Minister Zhao Ziyang who passed on to him the gist of the Chinese position that had just been secretly approved which was based on the 'one country two systems' formula that had been applied to Taiwan. But this was not sufficiently appreciated by a British side that was single-mindedly imbued with the idea that only a continued British administrative presence would ensure continued business confidence in Hong Kong following the reversion of sovereignty to China. This was all the more striking since in his book Cradock acknowledged that the Chinese 'concept of sovereignty embraced administration and from the outset they had been nonplussed by the distinction we drew'.[15] Moreover, in the wake of the victory in the Falklands, Mrs Thatcher was not easily persuaded that sovereignty should be given up.[16]

In other words, British misunderstandings and an insufficient appreciation of the significance of sovereignty to China's leaders undoubtedly deepened Chinese suspicions. In his meeting with Mrs Thatcher in September 1982, Deng Xiaoping claimed that there was a provision in the Hong Kong budget for transferring surplus capital directly to the British treasury. Although he was promptly disabused of that false information by the late Sir Edward Youde, there is every sign that he and the other senior Chinese leaders believe that the main British interest in Hong Kong is to extract large sums of money.[17] Cradock has said that the Chinese side believed that the British had such an economic interest in the territory that, if only he would let them know what the British side wanted, that would then be arranged and everything could then run smoothly. Meanwhile, Deng had instructed his negotiators, 'Watch those British lest they grab Hong Kong's capital'.[18]

Every turn in the negotiations has been dogged by Chinese suspicion of possible British schemes to secrete vast sums from Hong Kong. The provisions of Annex III of the Joint Declaration on Land Leases, including the establishment of the Land Commission, may be seen as illustrative of the Chinese concern that the British may sell off Government real estate in the territory so as to take away capital at the expense of the incoming administration of 1997. Similarly, the Chinese questioning of the major new airport project may be seen as demonstrating their fears that Britain may offer lucrative contracts to British firms or to firms with significant British interests that would in effect drain off Hong Kong's spare capital and its reserves, thereby leaving the post British administration with vast debts. Hence, the Memorandum of Understanding of July 1991 specifically obliged the (British) Hong Kong authorities to leave financial reserves of at least HK $25 billion for the new administration in 1997. The issue continued to delay further developments on the airport well into the following year and it has become thoroughly embroiled with the dispute over the Patten proposals. Consider, for example, Premier Li Peng's response to Governor Chris Patten's remarks that the projected airport should be seen as a 'dowry' bequeathed by the departing

British rather than as the financial millstone portrayed by the Chinese side: Li is reported to have said,

> During the more than one hundred years of its role, which began in 1884 [sic], the British Empire took away much more wealth than the 'dowry' it will leave in 1997.

He added that the airport's cost was too high and that it would bring financial difficulties to the territory after 1997.[19]

British policies on the Hong Kong issue have not only been shaped by a sense of moral responsibility for the welfare of the people of Hong Kong, but they have also been fuelled by a sense of guilt. As Britain's last major colony, its people are perhaps better qualified by education and by achievement to govern themselves than probably any other colony granted independence since the Second World War. Yet they are to be handed to the authority of a dictatorial government that in the 1950s and 1960s was responsible by its own admissions for the callous deaths of millions of its citizens. The hopes that it had undergone a fundamental change in the 1980s were dashed by the vivid scenes on television of the Chinese army killing demonstrators on the streets of Beijing on 4 June 1989. The sense of guilt by British ministers and officials has been deepened because of the denial by Parliament to at least 3.5 million British passport holders in Hong Kong of the right to reside in Britain. Consequently, British policy has been designed to leave the people of Hong Kong with as best a chance to exercise autonomy so as to preserve their way of life after the reversion to Chinese sovereignty. The differences between some senior British officials since 1992 have been over the best means to achieve this and the extent to which the opinions of Hong Kong people should be weighed in the balance against the need to cooperate with Beijing. But there should be no doubt that, all the way through, British policy towards Hong Kong has been shaped by this moral obligation. Perhaps, uniquely in British foreign policy, British fundamental interests such as cultivating better relations with China and promoting British commerce have been sacrificed time and again for a moral cause that at the end of the day may yield Britain precious little.[20]

Not surprisingly, this has never been appreciated or accepted by China's leaders. Indeed, more broadly, few intellectuals in Beijing could understand why so much emphasis had been placed on democracy when Hong Kong had seemed to operate perfectly well for so long without it.[21] Long before Governor Patten announced his proposals of political reforms, questions had been raised in China about the reasons for the British insistence on democratising Hong Kong. As early as 1985 Beijing expressed the view that representative government was being introduced not for the purpose of preserving the framework needed for a capitalist system, but in order 'to use democracy to resist communism' (*minzhu kang gong*).[22] In August 1992 (i.e. before Governor Patten had even worked out his proposals), a senior Chinese researcher explained that the Chinese government feared that Britain could 'cause trouble' by encouraging Hong Kong to become 'too independent' and that Hong Kong could become 'too strong' with 'too many independent institutions'.[23] If no commercial interest could be seen to be served by a particular British policy, the Chinese side tended to see ulterior purposes and dark conspiracies at work. Thus, China's leaders attributed the appointment of the senior politician, Chris Patten, and the announcement of his proposals to an allegedly long-standing British practice of destabilising colonies.[24] Still others saw a link between Patten and his proposals on the one hand, and, on the other, the support given to them by Western governments, the arms sales to Taiwan by the French and the Americans, and even the election of President Clinton as evidence of a coordinated campaign to undermine communism in China.[25]

Time and again it is evident that China's leaders see the world as dominated by the considerations of power and state interests including both material economic interests and governmental concerns to stay in office. The idea that the British would be motivated by concerns for the welfare of the *Chinese* people of Hong Kong whose interests they have claimed to understand and better represent than the Chinese government in Beijing would be dismissed as absurd. Chinese commentators and scholars claimed to be puzzled in September 1994 by the fact that, alone of the Western powers, Britain did not seem to acknowledge China's greater standing in world affairs. Unlike the USA, who had conceded to China by renewing the favourable tariff conditions and de-linking them from the question of human rights, or unlike France, who had conceded to Beijing on the Taiwan question, or indeed unlike Germany, whose leader had gone out of his way to cultivate China, Britain by contrast had conceded nothing on Hong Kong. Attempts to explain that British policy on Hong Kong was conducted according to what was judged to be best for Hong Kong and that it was not affected by these larger considerations were greeted with incredulity. The same commentators and scholars nine months later in June 1995 explained the improvement that had taken place in Sino-British relations with reference to the sharp deterioration in Sino-American relations from which Britain was said to have disassociated itself (unlike the period after the Tiananmen incident of June 1989).[26]

These problems were accentuated by differences in the diplomatic styles of the two sides.[27] The Chinese side may be said to have a tradition of 'struggle diplomacy' and a preference for reaching agreements based on broad and vaguely worded principles. The British, by contrast, have a diplomatic tradition of setting out the separate interests in considerable detail so as to establish the points in common and where accommodations may be reached with a view to referring upwards to the highest authority major issues or points on which no basis for compromise could be found. As a result, in their dealings with the Chinese, the British side has been much better prepared on points of detail and on the legal niceties. The British have also tended to be more punctilious in respecting the confidentialities of the proceedings. The Chinese have displayed less command of detail and have sought to bring pressure by selective leaks and by being less bound by confidentiality. In short, both sets of negotiators have found their encounters to be difficult and, at times, bruising experiences.

THE PROBLEM OF THE STRUCTURE OF THE NEGOTIATIONS

Two key problems may be identified from a Chinese perspective. The first arose from allowing Britain excessive lassitude in managing the transition from 1984 to 1997; and the second from the deliberate exclusion of the people of Hong Kong from effective participation in the negotiations that determined their future. The first was a product of the way in which the Chinese negotiators had become prisoners to the 1984 deadline they had set for concluding the negotiations with Britain that led to the Joint Declaration. Because of delays caused by suspicions and misunderstandings, a great deal had to be agreed in the last few weeks.

At that point, Deng suddenly proposed the setting up of a Sino-British Joint Commission to oversee the handling of the transitionary period, especially during the final stages. In particular, he sought to exercise a high degree of surveillance over all aspects of the administration of Hong Kong including civil service appointments, fiscal and monetary policy, land sales and constitutional development. But under the pressure of time, Deng agreed at the last moment to accept a

British proposal that had been hurriedly prepared on the flight from London. Picking on a phrase in the original Chinese proposal that the new body should not be an organ of power, the British negotiators argued that the British Hong Kong administration should be allowed to govern and hence what was now called a Joint Liaison Group should be an organ of consultation and a place where agreements should be reached about implementing the Joint Declaration in practice. Moreover, it would not meet in Hong Kong to begin with and even later it would do so only on a rotating basis meeting alternately in London and Beijing.[28] This meant that considerable powers were left to the British side in preparing Hong Kong for the transition to Chinese sovereignty.

Ten years later, Chinese scholars specialising in their country's foreign policy acknowledged that, from Beijing's perspective, it had been a mistake to give up on the Joint Commission. They said that the Chinese side had not developed clear plans and it took a while to set up a preparatory framework for drafting the Basic Law. Thus, it was left to the newly appointed head of NCNA, Xu Jiatun, to call a halt to what were regarded as unacceptable British plans to hasten the introduction of western style democracy to Hong Kong. China then developed the strategy of insisting that all major constitutional changes should be put off until after the publication of the Basic Law.

In this way, the Chinese side once again seized the momentum that had seemed to slide away immediately after the signing of the Joint Declaration. British negotiators at that point took the view that they had little alternative but to comply as China was immeasurably more powerful and could, if it chose, impose a unilateral solution. However, when Governor Patten took a different approach, he in effect seized the momentum from the Chinese side. By concentrating their ire upon him in a series of vitriolic abuse, China's leaders evidently thought that they could have him replaced by exerting sufficient pressure on what they judged to be the domestically weak government of John Major. An official of the Foreign Office privately confirmed that that was the Chinese view and, for good measure, they had hinted that they would make some concessions if he were to be recalled. When that did not work, the Chinese came forward with their 'second stove' and confirmed their threat to abolish the Legislative Council which, in their view, had not been established in accordance with the Basic Law. This high risk strategy may be seen as the result of having 'mistakenly' conceded too much control to Britain because of having set a deadline that in the end did not work entirely in their interests.

The other key problem was the exclusion of any formal representation of the people of Hong Kong in the negotiations of their future. As seen from Beijing, unlike the situation in Taiwan, Hong Kong was in the control of a foreign power and therefore the retrocession of sovereignty was to be negotiated with that power – Britain. It was inconceivable that Britain, the external colonial power, could speak on behalf of the Chinese people of Hong Kong or that such local people who had been inducted into the governing institutions of the colonial authority could do so either. The Chinese took the view that the British could include anyone they chose to join their negotiating team, but even if Hong Kong people were selected they could not speak for anyone other than the British. Accordingly, they took exception when the late Sir Edward Youde, the former Governor, claimed to join the negotiations as representing Hong Kong interests, just as earlier they had objected when a Foreign Office Minister spoke of the three-legged stool of Beijing, London and Hong Kong.[29] Ten years later they were to insist that the Hong Kong Secretary for Constitutional Affairs could attend negotiations only as a part of the British team.

When it came to the setting-up of the Basic Law which was to determine the constitutional structure for the future Hong Kong Special Administrative Region (HKSAR), different considerations applied from the Chinese perspective. As this was a domestic matter it was right and proper that all shades of opinion within Hong Kong should be consulted. After all, the goal was that Hong Kong people should rule Hong Kong (*Gangren zhi Gang*) within the framework of Chinese sovereignty. Since there was a further aim (at that stage) of converging the political reforms of the (British) Hong Kong government with the arrangements for the HKSAR, the British government too was allowed to contribute to the deliberations, but only with Beijing on an exclusive and confidential basis with reference to reaching agreement on how the Legislative Council should be constituted before 1997.

From a British perspective, however, the exclusion of Hong Kong representation from participation in determining their future was flawed not only from a moral point of view, but from a practical standpoint too. During the negotiations leading to the Joint Declaration, a way was found of taking local opinion into account by involving the Executive Council, and a way was found to sound out public opinion about the acceptability of the Joint Declaration on the proviso that it could not be amended.[30] But the Joint Declaration stated that the future HKSAR would enjoy 'a high degree of autonomy' without clarifying what that was, although it was agreed that the legislature would be constituted by 'elections'. Britain was charged with the responsibility of not only continuing to secure continuing stability and prosperity in Hong Kong, but also to prepare it to be in a position to exercise the 'high degree of autonomy' and a legislature constituted by 'elections' for when the HKSAR should come into effect in 1997. It was not explained what was meant by 'a high degree of autonomy' or by 'elections'.

As Hong Kong became increasingly politicised, the British Hong Kong government came under pressure from within the territory and from Parliament in London to move more rapidly towards greater democracy and to increase governmental accountability. At the same time, such moves towards political reform were suspect in the eyes of Beijing. They were seen as attempts to impose a *fait accompli* before 1997 that would leave China no alternative but to accept Hong Kong as a 'separate political entity' unconstrained by the Central People's government.[31] By the terms of the Joint Declaration, Britain was pledged to cooperate with China through the consultation process as laid down in the provisions for the Joint Liaison Group. These called for closer consultations in the second half of the period leading up to 1997. Thus, the (British) Hong Kong government was subject to contradictory pressures that could not be addressed within the structure of the negotiations, on the one hand, from within Hong Kong to quicken the pace of democratisation and, on the other, from Beijing's representatives to conform with their plans as in the Basic Law. Since that did not take final shape until 1990, it meant that direct elections to the Legislative Council had to wait until 1991. That placed the British in difficulty as they had earlier intimated that they could take place in 1988. A much criticised public opinion survey got the government off the hook by showing that there was not a majority for any particular method of conducting elections in 1988.[32] Hong Kong was, in effect, subject to conflicting sources of authority which could not be resolved within the available negotiating structures.

The repercussions of the Tiananmen events of 1989 threw these problems into stark relief. In seeking to regain the confidence of the people of Hong Kong, one million of whom had demonstrated against the killings in Beijing, the then Governor, Sir David Wilson, took measures that he knew would alienate Beijing. These included introducing a bill of rights, issuing British passports for 50,000 heads of households (in fact, he had campaigned in London for many more) and embarking on a huge airport project. Within Hong Kong it was generally accepted that the future of the territory depended upon the future evolution of China itself. Consequently, no objections were raised at the time against the organisation designed to help the Beijing demonstrators headed by the leading democrats, Martin Lee and Szeto Wah. However, they were later denounced as subversives, actively engaged in trying to topple the communist regime itself. This contributed to the polarisation of views within Hong Kong. It also provided a context in which the advent of Chris Patten, as a governor determined to reflect the views of and aspirations of Hong Kong people and who was unfamiliar with China and its ways, exacerbated the underlying contradictions.

It should be recognised that despite the problems of 'Tiananmen', the British and Chinese sides found ways to cooperate in a number of important areas. Many practical matters affecting the commercial position of Hong Kong and its relations with the mainland have been quietly settled without fuss or publicity. For example, all the complex organisational aspects affecting the port, navigation, the movement of goods across the border etc., have been handled reasonably well. There are even good working relations between the security authorities on both sides of the border, although problems have occasionally arisen because of smuggling, in which corrupt security or military officers on the mainland have been involved. Nor have the Chinese raised any objection whatsoever to the representatives of the existing government formally occupying the Hong Kong seat at the GATT or the Asia Pacific Economic Cooperation forum and other international organisations (provided, of course, that these do not require sovereignty as a condition of membership). PRC representatives sit alongside those of Hong Kong without ever questioning the way in which they articulate the territory's interests or querying their right to do so. The only occasion in which the Chinese briefly raised an objection concerned the question of the attendance of Hong Kong's representative at the November 1993 summit that President Clinton had attached to the APEC meeting in Seattle. But that had more to do with Taiwan's representation and, once the issue of protocol had been settled to Beijing's satisfaction, the Hong Kong representative (the Financial Secretary) duly attended without mishap. Beijing has also raised no objection to the various Economic Trade Offices that Hong Kong has opened in important cities in the world. The one in Washington has at times played a political role, for example, in lobbying for the continuation of extending China's favourable tariff terms for its imports into the USA. Thus, the Chinese have proved to be quite flexible on several issues including international representation, as long as their sovereign claims have not been publicly challenged or their claims to speak on behalf of the people of Hong Kong openly contested. This has nevertheless had the effect of denying Hong Kong people a direct voice (other than an advisory one) in the determination of their political system while, at the same time, gradually building that system.

Beijing has all along enjoyed the unchallengeable power over Hong Kong and it could have afforded to take a more indulgent view. But its regime felt beleaguered in the post-Tiananmen period and, imbued with a sense of self-righteous nationalism, it no longer sought to compromise with its foe (the new Governor) of the territory it was impatient to recover. Goaded by his challenge, Beijing produced its 'second stove', formally committed itself to proceed with a provisional Legislative Council, and contributed to the polarisation of Hong Kong by refusing to deal with members of the Democrat Party even though the largest number of votes were cast for them in the two direct elections of 1991 and 1995. Yet, in the summer of 1995, Beijing found it in its interests to cooperate once again with Britain and the (British) government of Hong Kong. This culminated in a visit to London by Vice Premier and Foreign Minister Qian Qichen on 2–4 October. Both sides professed to be pleased with the outcome of the visit. Not only did it improve the atmosphere between them, but agreement was reached to provide an institutional form for enhancing their cooperation in the lead-up to 1 July 1997. The Hong Kong government would establish a liaison office to deal directly with the Preparatory Committee after its establishment in January 1996.

However, within a month the new mood was soured by Beijing's declaration through its nominees in the Preliminary Working Committee (PWC) of its intent to modify the Bill of Rights on the grounds that it allegedly contravenes the Basic Law. For good measure, Beijing also declared its intention to reintroduce six ordinances that had been on the books so as to deal with subversive and riotous challenges posed principally by leftists that the Hong Kong government had recently removed from the statutes. From Beijing's perspective, the main point at issue was not so much the legal niceties but the aversion of the Chinese side to be bound by measures to which it had not previously agreed, especially as these would have limited its scope to deal with what it regarded as potentially subversive democratic elements who had seemingly been encouraged by the outgoing

British. Chinese sensitivity on such an issue deemed to affect its sovereignty has been heightened by the tilt towards neoconservatism as evident in the Ninth Five Year Plan that was published around this time.[33] What was missing in the way that Beijing handled the issue was any consideration as to how this might be received in Hong Kong. Having declared its hand, Beijing refused to budge or to respond to the concern expressed by many groups in the territory, including those normally sympathetic to its interests. As a result, the Legislative Council voted on 15 November 1995 overwhelmingly (40:15) against what Beijing had in mind. Therefore, Beijing will probably leave the rescinding of the Bill of Rights to its proposed provisional LEGCO to be appointed in late 1996 or early 1997. The issue has been seen within Hong Kong as potentially damaging to confidence – that elusive but necessary condition for the territory's prosperity and stability. Beijing's capacity to impose a unilateral solution on Hong Kong has never been in doubt; the question has been how can Beijing regain sovereignty over Hong Kong without undermining confidence and damaging its many substantive interests in a smooth transfer of sovereignty. If ever a negotiating structure involving the so-called 'three legged stool' of London, Beijing and Hong Kong were needed, it would appear to be in the final period of the transition. This could be yet another case where nationalist ideology has stood in the way of a rational approach.

THE COMMONALITY OF INTERESTS

When questioned in 1992, before the new Governor, Chris Patten, had broadcast his proposals, the leading negotiators on both sides tended to play down the significance of perceptions, possible misunderstandings and organisational problems. Instead, they stressed the differences of interest. For example, Anthony Galsworthy (then head of the British side of the Joint Liaison Group) argued that differences and difficulties stemmed from conflicts of interest and the character of the Chinese political system. William Ehrman (then the Political Adviser to the Governor) claimed that Ji Pengfei (the former Foreign Minister and Director of the Hong Kong and Macao Affairs Office and then a member of the Communist Party's Foreign Affairs Leading Group) also had denied that anything other than a conflict of interest was involved between the two sides. Lu Ping (the Director of the Hong Kong and Macao Affairs Office) argued that the difference between the two sides was that the British had a 'short-term interest up until

1997', whereas the Chinese had a 'long-term interest in the situation after 1997'.[34] Later on in 1993 and 1994, Chinese officials and scholars put all the blame on Patten and talked up the cordiality of the previous decade of negotiations.[35]

The officials may well have been right to draw attention to differences between Chinese and British negotiating interests. However, from a longer perspective, these differences paled into insignificance in comparison to the shared interest of both countries in effecting a smooth transition of sovereignty that would enable Hong Kong to continue to flourish as a major international commercial centre based upon freedom under a proper system of law. Britain will have been seen to have discharged its moral responsibilities to the people of Hong Kong and it would benefit from the resulting goodwill in relations with China and, indeed, within the Asia-Pacific as a whole. The consequences of failure would be correspondingly damaging. That could lead to the collapse of confidence followed by a break-down of order and the flight of a new wave of refugees – what the previous Governor, now Lord Wilson, called the 'Armageddon scenario'. A public disaster of that magnitude would inevitably affect the standing of the British government at home and abroad, hurting its prestige in the eyes of allies and undermining Britain's relations with China and much of the rest of East Asia. China's gains and losses, as were examined in Chapter 1, are potentially of a far greater magnitude as they could enhance or destroy much of the country's strategy for economic development as well as affect (for good or for ill) policy towards Taiwan. Beyond that, the repercussions for China's foreign relations in the Asia-Pacific would be immense.

Viewed in this light, it is not surprising that despite all the difficulties and the depth of distrust, the two sides were able to reach important agreements in 1994–1995 that broke the log jam on military lands, the Court of Final Appeal and the airport. The continuing danger is not that competing interests should intrude, but rather that their systemic differences and misunderstandings allied to the flaws in the structure of the negotiations should prevent Beijing, London and Hong Kong from arranging the smooth transfer of sovereignty and continuities in the Hong Kong way of life that their common interests all require.

Chapter 4

Problems of the last phase of transition

The final run-up to the reversion of sovereignty was always going to be the most sensitive and difficult part of the transition. In order to understand the Chinese perspective, it is important to evaluate the general Chinese approach to the problem. In particular, consideration must be given first to the ways in which the Chinese side organised itself for the task; second, to the problems involved in cooperating with British; and, most importantly, to how they cultivated ties with the people of Hong Kong. As seen from the perspective of people in Hong Kong, moving from a British-based administration whose practices were known, understood and trusted, to one whose authority derived from Beijing was bound to be a troublesome and uncertain process. Bereft of natural resources, Hong Kong depended upon the confidence of its own people in their system of government and upon the confidence of others in its capacities to act as an international financial centre and its abilities to serve as a gateway to China. These, in turn, depended upon continued trust in the efficiency of its civil service, the probity of its rule of law and the free flow of information and ideas. The international business community held none of these in high regard with respect to China itself. Whether or not these concerns and their implications were fully recognised in Beijing, China's leaders realised at an early stage that closer cooperation with Britain would be desirable, especially in the latter stage of the transition. Generally, however, China's leaders did not seem unduly worried as they held that it was the success of the economy on the mainland that provided the conditions for the success of Hong Kong and that there was no question that Chinese people were sufficiently capable of running Hong Kong. But the Chinese tendency to avoid detailed commitments and plan ahead with little more than broad prescriptions was disquieting, even though it also allowed for considerable flexibility.

There has continued to be the abiding problem of Chinese distrust of the British. As seen by Deng Xiaoping at the time of negotiating the Joint Declaration in 1984, extra vigilance would be needed as 1997 approached to ensure that the departing British would not take away 'the family silver' of Hong Kong, or leave the place in a mess in the hands of pro-British elements.[1] Beyond these dark suspicions, little thought appears to have been devoted to the problems of the transition itself. Indeed, the British negotiators confessed themselves surprised to find out how little the Chinese had prepared once it had been decided in the autumn of 1983 to explore their proposals for the future of Hong Kong.[2] Even when the Chinese side in 1990 finally sketched out their scheme for the future HKSAR in the form of the Basic Law, considerable uncertainties remained both about the process of the transition and about the vagueness in law of some of the terms used in the Basic Law and about its own institutional arrangements with the future HKSAR. In the view of many within Hong Kong, the vagueness of the Basic Law will provide a legal basis for the central government to exercise considerable control over the internal affairs of the HKSAR in addition to those of defence and foreign affairs.

Chinese approaches to people in Hong Kong seemed to many to show evidence of a desire to establish controls rather than to allow for a proper kind of autonomy. The selection of Hong Kong personnel to serve on the Preliminary Working Committee and an even larger number to serve as designated 'advisers' drew on a broad range of opinion in Hong Kong. But the Democrats, who have been shown to enjoy majority support in every election in the territory, were excluded and the selection was weighted in favour of people considered to be 'pro-China'. Given the Chinese determination to proceed with its provisional legislature, the Chinese discrimination against the most popular political party was seen as disturbing and divisive. Hong Kong was being polarised by people being classified as 'pro-China' or 'pro-British'. It was becoming more difficult to articulate what might be called a 'pro-Hong Kong' position. Such a position would call for preserving the existing institutions and freedoms as being necessary for the continuation of the territory's role as an international business centre that alone would enable Hong Kong to continue to play its vital role in serving the Chinese motherland. In other words, the 'pro-Hong Kong' position would claim to be the truly patriotic one. It would assert that, although the institutions of the territory had been put in place initially by the British, they were made to work by the people of Hong Kong and in that process they had acquired features unique to the territory. They were no longer British, but they were 'Hong Kongese', perhaps in a way analogous to the way the Chinese Communist Party was Chinese despite the Germanic and Russian origins of communism itself.

In other words, what has been called here 'the Hong Kong position' would not recognise that a contradiction existed between standing up for Hong Kong and being patriotic. On the contrary, in this view it would be against China's best interests to allow the distinctive Hong Kong system to be eroded in a vain attempt to please China's leaders in the short run. Indeed, it can be argued that the attempt to polarise the people of Hong Kong into 'pro-China' and 'pro-British' groups has been self-defeating. It has hampered the development of the CCP's traditional united front strategy of winning over all those who could be won over so as to isolate true opponents in the minority. It has been perceived as a divisive and intimidatory tactic. Its result was evident in the Legislative Council elections of September 1995 when the 'pro-Chinese' candidates fared unexpectedly badly and the supposedly 'pro-British' candidates triumphed, out-voting the former by margins of 2:1 and even 3:1. The result has been to expose a wide gulf between Beijing and the bulk of the middle class professionals. It is this group which forms the backbone for the financial and other modern services that have become central to the contemporary economy of Hong Kong. Hundreds of thousands of these people possess foreign passports and the right of residence abroad. It would be a disaster for the territory if they were to be so alienated from the incoming sovereign power and so despairing of its understanding of the way that Hong Kong works that they should feel impelled to leave.

THE ORGANISATIONAL ARRANGEMENTS FOR THE TRANSITION

The Chinese, in effect, pushed all the crucial arrangements that they had to make into the last 18 months of the transition. Thus, according to the decisions taken by China's National People's Congress which approved the Basic Law on 4 April 1990, a Preparatory Committee made up of mainland and Hong Kong members (who will constitute at least half the membership) will be appointed by the NPC 'within the year 1996'. This will in turn nominate a Selection Committee of 400 permanent residents of Hong Kong who must be broadly representative and who will recommend a candidate for Chief Executive of the future HKSAR for appointment by the Central People's Government. Since it was decided in 1993 to establish a provisional Legislative Council (for which no provisions were made in the Basic Law), it was also decided that the Preparatory Committee will select the members for that too. It will be noted that no date was specified by which these selections should be made. The NPC also decided that in the event of the Legislative Council (in existence before July 1997) having been constituted according to the Basic Law, the Preparatory Committee would also confirm whether its members qualified to serve on the first HKSAR Legislative Council. But since Beijing claims that the 1995 elections contravene the Basic Law, this last task for the Preparatory Committee presumably no longer applies.

In practice, however, the Chinese authorities have left all their options open. They have not formally explained by what criteria members for the Preparatory Committee will be chosen. It is generally assumed in Hong Kong that these will be drawn from the existing members of the Preliminary Working Committee that was appointed in advance of the Preparatory Committee in 1993. Those selected as 'advisers' on Hong Kong to the Chinese government could also be selected. But it is entirely possible that the Chinese authorities could cast their net wider in the interests of demonstrating a truly broad representation of Hong Kong people. Since up to fifty per cent of the membership can be drawn from the mainland, Beijing would have little difficulty in ensuring that, if necessary, it could command an effective majority in the Committee.

Beijing has also assured itself of a broad room for manoeuvre on the question of the Legislative Council. As the Xinhua Branch in Hong Kong was openly active in supporting the electoral campaigns of what were regarded as 'pro-China' candidates, the Chinese authorities could choose to find merit in some, if not all, of the Legislative Councillors elected directly or indirectly in September 1995. Indeed, the Chinese authorities have not excluded the options of allowing all, some or none of these members to serve on the provisional legislature. Moreover, it is not at all clear when the members of the provisional body will be selected. This could be done in, say, September 1996 on the grounds that it would be more conducive to stability if the membership were known well in advance of the transfer of sovereignty. On the other hand, it could be delayed until much nearer 1 July 1997 so as to minimise the confusion that might result from possibly undermining the authority of the existing Council. It would also complicate the work of the civil service and, indeed, of the Chief Executive designate.

The process of the appointment of the Chief Executive is less clear even though it was specifically spelt out in the decisions of the NPC of 4 April 1990 which approved the Basic Law. The Preparatory Committee will choose a 400-member Selection Committee 'composed entirely of permanent residents of Hong Kong' who will be 'broadly representative'. This committee will then 'recommend the candidate through local consultations or through nomination and election after consultations, and report the recommended candidate to the Central Government for appointment'. The NPC decision did not specify when the appointment would be made, but it implied that it should be in good time before 1 July 1997 as it charged the Chief Executive with the responsibility of 'preparing for the formation of the first government'. Since then, Beijing has indicated that the Chief Executive designate should be nominated by the summer of 1996 in order to enable him or her to become familiar with the work of the government so as to make the appropriate senior appointments and be adequately prepared by 1 July 1997.

Once selected, presumably in the summer of 1996, the Chief Executive designate will be expected to prepare for the government of the SAR by becoming familiar with the machinery of government that will be continued beyond 1 July 1997 and by selecting the key personnel who will be of assistance in first preparing and then executing the agenda for the SAR government once the transfer of sovereignty takes place. The transitionary period, however, will be fraught with difficulties. Unlike the arrangements in Washington, when the outgoing president (according to custom) assists the newly-elected successor to get used to the Presidency as he perseveres to the moment of the latter's assumption of office, there is no such custom in Hong Kong. Although the last colonial Governor has pledged to cooperate with the future Chief Executive designate and to offer such assistance as may be requested, it will be difficult. Not only is Chris Patten reviled and distrusted by Chinese officials, but cooperation will also be hampered by their different loyalties and sources of accountability. The Colonial Governor is ultimately accountable to London, whereas the Chief Executive will be answerable to both Hong Kong and Beijing. The Governor will be responsible for the administration of the territory right until the transfer of sovereignty and he could hardly share that with what, in effect, is Beijing's nominee. By the same token, it is unlikely that the Chief Executive will want to be too closely associated with the Governor's executive actions either. At best the one could help the other to understand better the complex procedures involved in making policy and overseeing its implementation. But even in this regard complications may arise about the role of the Legislative Council in the governmental process since the SAR will be expected to start with a different provisional council. The Chief Executive designate's role in the transitionary period will be further complicated by the continued operations of the HKMAO and the NCNA Hong Kong Branch who, doubtless, will still have much to say about the present and future workings of the territory.

The Chief Executive will possess many of the extraordinary powers enjoyed by British governors down the years. According to the Basic Law (Article 48), they include: leading the HKSAR government; being responsible for signing bills into law and for implementing them; signing budgets; deciding on government policies and issuing directives; appointing and removing senior officials (subject to the endorsement of the Central Government); appointing and removing judges; and approving the introduction of motions regarding revenues or expenditure to the Legislative Council. The Chief Executive will also be accountable to the Central Government as well as to the HKSAR and will be required to report to it and carry out its instructions in accordance with the Basic Law. It is inconceivable that Beijing would leave such a crucial nomination to be determined by Hong Kong people alone, as specified in the NPC decision of 4 April 1995.

In fact, it is generally understood in Hong Kong that in practice it is Beijing that will decide. But as to how and on what basis Beijing will do so is obscure. In early 1995 some scholars in Beijing claimed that the central leaders wanted someone whom they could trust; someone who, at the same time, would enjoy the confidence of the business, civil service, legal, professional and other communities in Hong Kong; someone who would be a high-profile figure, respected internationally, who would enjoy the confidence of the international financial community. When asked as to whether any such person existed, they freely confessed that they did not know of one. When pressed, these scholars conceded that it was highly unlikely that a senior member of the Chinese Communist Party would be suitable as he or she would lack the appropriate experience and would probably not enjoy the confidence of people in Hong Kong or the international financial community. Moreover, they pointed out that it was unlikely that a senior party member would qualify as, according to the Basic Law (Article 44), the Chief Executive should have 'ordinarily resided in Hong Kong for a continuous period of not less than 20 years.'[3]

If the Chief Executive designate is unlikely to be a senior member of the CCP, the question arises as to how the CCP will be represented in the last transitional phase and beyond. Since 1949, the Xinhua News Agency Hong Kong Branch has served as both the representative of the CCP and the Central Government. It could not continue to function and be constituted in its present form beyond the end of the British presence without undermining or appearing to undermine the authority of the HKSAR and its Chief Executive. It could not continue to be the representative of the Central Government and, indeed, its official voice in Hong Kong alongside a local (albeit a formally autonomous) government that was subordinate to that Central Government without being an alternative source of authority. But if the Xinhua Branch were to shed its formal governmental role while seeking to uphold its position as the head of the CCP in the HKSAR, that too would contribute to damaging the authority of the Chief Executive before too long. It would soon become apparent that real power was located there if only because of the leading position of the CCP in Beijing.

CHINESE DECISION-MAKING ON HONG KONG

Before exploring further the question of future CCP representation in Hong Kong, it is first necessary to consider the organisations through which China's policies towards Hong Kong have been carried out. The formal negotiations with Britain have been conducted under the auspices of the West European Division of the Ministry of Foreign Affairs (MFA). The Hong Kong and Macao Affairs Office that was set up in 1978 has been responsible for carrying out investigations and sounding out views in Hong Kong and China before passing on its policy recommendations to the higher leaders. Its head enjoys ministerial status and reports directly to the State Council (more specifically the Prime Minister). The Hong Kong Branch of Xinhua News Agency (or NCNA) was set up in 1948 and, as we have seen, it formally represents the Central Government and the CCP. Its lines of communication to Beijing are complex and unclear. Its head, Zhou Nan, has ministerial status, and the NCNA is the office through which the local representative of the British Foreign Office (the Political

Adviser) communicates with the Chinese government. The communication is with a branch of the NCNA called the Agency-Work Committee of the communist party. It reports to the Hong Kong and Macao Office within the Ministry of Foreign Affairs and also to the Foreign Affairs Leading Small Group of the Central Committee – the leading foreign policy-making body in the country. But in its capacity as the local branch of the official news agency, it is also part of the Xinhua News Agency which enjoys ministerial status in the Central Government.

However, the primary role of the NCNA has been its position as the 'Hong Kong and Macau Work Committee of the Communist Party of China'. It is linked to several important departments of the Central Committee including Propaganda, United Front and International Liaison. The Propaganda Department, as its name suggests, seeks to uphold communist ideals and cultural values within China and to determine the message that China presents to the outside world. The Hong Kong Branch with its control of two key newspapers has been an important outpost. Among other matters, the United Front Department has sought to cultivate relations with other social classes and Chinese Overseas. The International Liaison Department used to be concerned with relations with other communist parties and Hong Kong was an important 'listening post' for links with parties engaged in armed struggle in Southeast Asia. Since the CCP abandoned support for such activities in the late 1970s, the significance of that department for the Hong Kong NCNA presumably came to an end. With a personnel of more than 500, the NCNA contains many bureaus, including policy research, finance, trade, united front, propaganda, economics, culture, education, sports and social (youth and women's) work, the arts and foreign affairs as well as conventional media activities. Additionally, it provides staff for the Chinese representatives of the Sino-British Joint Liaison Group.[4]

All three organisations – the MFA, the HKMAO and the NCNA (Hong Kong Branch) – were formally under the leadership of State Council and the Foreign Affairs Small Group of the Central Committee.[5] A retired vice-secretary general of NCNA explained in June 1994:

> The Foreign Minister Qian Qichen, as a politburo member, handles foreign affairs, Hong Kong and Macao, and Taiwan. As the assistant of Jiang Zemin and Li Peng, Qian helps with Hong Kong. So Jiang and Li are the highest power-holders in respect of

Hong Kong. Right now, matters of great importance concerning Hong Kong is [*sic*] first reported to Qian, then Jiang and Li are asked for advice. Jiang and Li divide Hong Kong between them: Li handles most jobs concerning government departments, while Jiang handles party affairs and decisions concerning the overall situation. It can be said that Jiang handles more than Li . . . Xinhua is the top level overseas post of the Chinese Communist party, while the Hong Kong and Macau Affairs Office is an office of the State Council.[6]

But it is important to recognise that, at the highest levels of leadership, personal power and the influence of personal networks tended to count for more than rigidly-defined institutional divisions of labour. In other words, the personal standing of individuals within the Party has been a more accurate guide to effective power and influence than formal official positions in the hierarchy. Liao Chengzhi, for example, who was the first head of the HKMAO which he led from 1978 until his untimely death in 1983, exercised far greater influence than any of his successors. Liao was an old associate of Mao Zedong and Zhou Enlai who was trusted by them to negotiate with the Japanese in the 1960s. He was closely connected with the Chinese Overseas and he enjoyed close relations with Deng Xiaoping. Thus, he was entrusted with drafting the so-called '12 Points' in 1981 which defined the application of Deng's 'one country two systems' scheme to Hong Kong and became the basis for the agreement with Britain in 1984.[7]

The most important leadership on the handling of Hong Kong has been provided by none other than Deng Xiaoping himself. It was an issue in which he not only took a personal interest, but over which he exercised direct command and control. This was evident to the British negotiators as he took all the major decisions and determined the turning points in the negotiations. Thus, in the negotiations leading to the Joint Declaration, he met all the key British ministers, set the ultimatum and the deadline, first proposed a joint commission and then relented in favour of a looser consultative Joint Liaison Group, and finally agreed to the horse-trading in the last few days that settled the agreement.[8] Unusually, Deng Xiaoping showed his personal responsibility in public on several occasions. Perhaps the most surprising of these was his public rebuke to the former Defence Minister Geng Biao and former Foreign Minister Huang Hua for suggesting in 1984 that it would not be necessary to station the

Chinese army in Hong Kong itself.[9] Deng's personal role has also been given an ideological significance by the separate publication of nine of his articles from his *Selected Works*, Vol. III, under the title *Deng Xiaoping on the Question of Hong Kong*.[10]

From the perspective of the Central Government in Beijing, Deng Xiaoping's personal control of the Hong Kong question meant that other bureaucracies did not become directly involved. It also had the effect of limiting the initiative that those charged with administering the policies could display. The only official to display initiative was Xu Jiatun – head of NCNA in Hong Kong from 1983 until 1990. As a former Party secretary of Jiangsu Province, he was a senior member of the Central Committee and was trusted by the Party hierarchy. His initiative took the form of cultivating the different groups in Hong Kong, while at the same time upholding Beijing's interests in limiting the democratisation in Hong Kong to the constraints of the yet to be completed Basic Law. In time, however, he came to understand Hong Kong perhaps too well and in the aftermath of the Tiananmen killings of June 1989 he left the following year for the United States. The NCNA that he left behind had been badly divided by the Tiananmen events. His replacement, Zhou Nan, lacked the Party seniority, but as a leading negotiator with the British he had earned the reputation of being tough and unyielding. He imposed order within the NCNA and in comparison with his predecessor he did not seek to cultivate contacts within Hong Kong. He gained the reputation of being a 'leftist' and of someone who could be guaranteed to identify ulterior purposes behind any British proposal.

With his formal retirement in 1989, Deng Xiaoping's interventions in Chinese politics tended to be conducted through his private office. As he aged, he came to depend increasingly upon his secretary and his daughters to mediate between him and others. Indeed, as he became incapacitated by his advanced age his personal direction of Hong Kong affairs became more of a liability than an asset. His interventions became more erratic and, according to British side, there was a tendency for the lesser officials engaged in Hong Kong matters to take the 'safer' approaches of either doing nothing or taking an unyielding 'leftist' nationalist line.[11] Indeed, it was not until after Deng finally became politically inactive around November 1994 that other senior leaders began to voice a public interest in Hong Kong.

Party General Secretary Jiang Zemin and Prime Minister Li Peng had in the past spoken in public, but they were acknowledged to exercise formal bureaucratic responsibilities for the territory. Jiang was head of the Party's Foreign Affairs Small Group and Li was head of the State Council. But early in the new year Qiao Shi, head of the NPC, saw fit to give a public reassurance that the Hong Kong economy would be all right as long as the economy of the mainland continued to perform well.[12] More significantly, Li Ruihuan, the head of the Political Consultative Conference (as mentioned in Chapter 2), publicly warned the Chinese side to take care in their dealing with Hong Kong as there was much that was not understood about its workings.[13] Qiao and Li spoke as leaders of representative institutions which included people from Hong Kong as members. But the fact that they had not done so before suggested that it was only once Deng Xiaoping had ceased to be politically active from the end of 1994 that they were able to speak out on Hong Kong. Moreover, by asserting their claims to have a say in the resolution of the Hong Kong question they were also bringing it to the fore as an issue for the collective leadership as a whole. Unlike Li Peng who tended to take a harder line on the issue perhaps arising out of his institutional interests, Qiao Hi and Li Ruihuan were also more flexible. Qiao, as head of the law-making and key representative body, the NPC, had an institutional interest in promoting greater legality in China. Li, as head of the key united front organisation, had an institutional interest in being receptive to the concerns of Hong Kong people. As members of the seven-man Standing Committee of the Politburo, they were not only showing that China was moving towards a collective style of leadership as the post-Deng Xiaoping era approached, but they were also signalling that the handling of the Hong Kong question could be a factor in the manoeuvring and the jockeying for position that will follow the announcement of the death of Deng Xiaoping.

THE 1995 TURNING POINT

If Deng's increasing incapacity had an immobilising effect, as long as he could still issue key announcements from time to time, his final loss of coherence seemed to push his putative successors into making a few key decisions. Deng's successors, decided in the politburo meeting of March 1995 to take a more cooperative approach towards the British.[14] As if to signal Deng's new stage of incoherence, a photograph of a dazed and senile looking Deng Xiaoping taken on 1 October 1994 was released to the Hong Kong press in late February 1995 and was also published by the Party newspaper in Shanghai.[15] It was after that decision that Li Ruihuan made his important speech on

13 March. Later that summer in June, agreements were finally reached with Britain on the Court of Final Appeal and on the financing of the airport. Qian Qichen (Vice Premier, Foreign Minister and head of the Preliminary Working Committee for Hong Kong), Lu Ping (head of HKMAO) and Zhou Nan (head of the NCNA Hong Kong) all separately went out of their way to assure civil servants in Hong Kong who had found their earlier statements disturbing.[16] In early July this was followed by a secret visit to Beijing by Anson Chan, Chief Secretary in Hong Kong and deputy to the Governor. In the past, she had been ostracised as a member of the colonial establishment, but it was recalled that her grandfather had been a revolutionary martyr and, in the course of her three-day visit (described as personal), she discussed the future of Hong Kong with Qian Qichen and Lu Ping. The Governor, Chris Patten, commented that 'indirectly, talking to the chief secretary, anyone is talking to me as well'.[17]

The decision to cooperate with Britain over Hong Kong that was taken in the Spring of 1995 should be understood within a wider context. It is illustrative of the contrast between Chinese and British approaches to the question. Whereas the British have tended to treat Hong Kong in a separate niche from the rest of its foreign policy, the Chinese have tended to treat it as part of a much broader domestic and international canvass. As discussed in Chapter 3, Britain's interests are focused entirely on managing a smooth transfer of sovereignty that will preserve Hong Kong's way of life and that will be acceptable to its people. The Chinese authorities are not only determined to re-establish sovereignty, they seek to do so in ways that will not lead to the subversion of their politics, that will help them in the reunification with Taiwan, and that will serve their broad foreign policy goals in the Asia-Pacific, as well as in ways that will serve the economy. Deng Xiaoping's successors have an additional incentive in handling the reversion of sovereignty in that it will be the first big test of their effectiveness as leaders.

Several factors were involved in reaching the decision. In particular, as the clock facing Tiananmen Square graphically illustrated, the time was fast approaching when sovereignty would be resumed. The clock was first displayed after the Legislative Council, in disregard of Chinese objections, had voted into law Patten's proposals for electoral reform on 30 June 1994. But from being a warning to the people of Hong Kong, the clock had begun to 'tick' for Beijing too. It became a graphic reminder that the resumption of sovereignty and taking this new step towards national reunification involved matters of the highest prestige that the new leaders would have to manage well and manage soon. Unlike most of China's other problems that were deep set and not susceptible to rapid solutions, the resolution of the Hong Kong question was fixed in the calender and the new leaders would be judged by how well they took care of the restoration of sovereignty. In addition, many important and practical issues depended on a successful management of Hong Kong. These included considerable implications for the domestic economy, ramifications for foreign economic relations, and the demonstrative implications for the people of Taiwan of applying the scheme of 'one country two systems' to Hong Kong. Time was short and because so much of the work of the transition had been left to be carried out in the remaining two years, it made sense to see whether closer cooperation with Britain was possible. As Li Ruihuan had suggested to the Hong Kong representatives, there was much about the way of life and the running of the territory that China still had to learn. If it were not handled well, Hong Kong could be damaged – like an ancient tea pot – even as a result of good intentions.

At this point, it is important to take into account the international context. Since the high point of the summer of 1994, relations with the USA and Japan had begun to deteriorate. The Chinese had found that the American business corporations who had been so useful over the MFN issue in exerting pressure on the US president were unwilling to do so over China's entry into the World Trade Organization, or over the question of protecting Intellectual Property Rights. The Chinese had to climb down over the latter in February 1995, but they still encountered American pressure on a range of questions. Although many observers argued that the foreign policy process in America was in disarray, on issue after issue the USA took positions that opposed Chinese interests.[18] China's leaders concluded that they were subject to a concerted American policy aimed against them. Singapore's Senior Minister Lee Kuan Yew reported in August 1995 that President Jiang Zemin and Premier Li Peng had separately told of their 'feeling that it was US policy to contain China, to block or slow down its economic progress and growth as a power'.[19] American attempts to upgrade relations with Taiwan (evident even before the granting of a visa to Taiwan's President Lee Teng-hui in early June 1995) were regarded as supportive of the independence tendencies in Taiwan and, therefore, as indicative of a desire to split the Chinese nation.[20] Relations with Japan, too, had declined since the high points of 1993/1994 when Japanese investment had soared and it had become China's leading trade partner. Towards the end of 1994, it was evident that Japanese investment was declining and that the Japanese government was becoming more critical of China because of its failure to become more open about its military developments and because of its continued testing of nuclear weapons. More generally, within Japan there was evidence of unease about China's growing significance in the Asia-Pacific.[21]

But unlike the situation that obtained after the Tiananmen killings of 4 June 1989, the European Union countries and Britain in particular did not seem to be following American policy on China. The British, like their European allies, did not support American unilateralism on trade matters and they pursued human rights questions in a less openly confrontational way. Moreover, the British were still seen as a declining power who could not obstruct China's growing significance. It made sense, therefore, from Beijing's perspective to try and improve relations with the European countries so as to avoid the development of antagonistic relations with all the western powers at the same time. Better relations with the Europeans should also increase the room for diplomatic manoeuvre with the USA. At the same time, the Chinese government sought to scale down the conflict with Southeast Asian countries over the Spratlys. At the August meeting of the ASEAN Regional Forum, the Chinese Foreign Minister Qian Qichen offered for the first time to deal with the conflict within the framework of International Law and, in particular, the Law of the Sea.[22] It was hoped that it would stop the Americans from being drawn into the conflict, especially as they had expressed their interest in ensuring that the sea lanes in the South China Sea should be kept open and secure. The Chinese side also sought to establish means of cooperation with the Philippines in joint activities to monitor the weather, handle problems of fishing, smuggling and piracy. They hoped that once cooperation was achieved in these fields, they could be extended to the more contentious area of resource development and, meanwhile, such examples of cooperation could be used as models for Chinese cooperation with other countries.[23]

However, once having established the desirability of cooperation with Britain over Hong Kong, it remained for China's leaders to be convinced that it was feasible. In their view, Governor Patten and the British government had violated previous agreements and had undermined the previous basis for cooperation between the two sides. Indeed, the most important part of Patten's programme to which the

Chinese side objected so strongly was due to take place later that year in September – the elections to the Legislative Council under the terms of his new franchise. But a number of considerations came into play. First, it had already proved possible to reach agreements on non-constitutional matters after Patten had passed his electoral ·bill through the Legislative Council in 1994, for example, over the use of military lands and over the financing of the controversial airport. Second, the British were proving to be more cooperative than had previously been the case, especially with reference to the Preliminary Working Committee. Patten had been relatively conciliatory towards it in his annual statement in October 1994. But the turning point was Patten's unilateral acceptance of the proposals put forward by the PWC for the Court of Final Appeal that opened the door to an agreement on that issue and then finally to the last necessary arrangements required by international investors for backing the financing of the airport.

Apparently, the breakthrough agreement on the Court of Final Appeal came as a surprise to the British side. This had been deadlocked since the Legislative Council had turned down the agreement between Britain and China over the issue in 1991. Intending to have the Court up and running before the transfer of sovereignty so as to complete the necessary arrangements for the rule of law beyond 30 June 1997, the British side made further proposals to the Chinese side with the intention of proceeding unilaterally if no agreement could be reached. The Chinese did not respond until the British were on the verge of putting their proposals before the Legislative Council. At the last moment a response was received through the legal section of the PWC. A few uncontested principles were put forward by the PWC. This was seen as an attempt to shift the blame on Britain for proceeding unilaterally. As part of the 'propaganda war' the British responded in kind only to find to their surprise that the Chinese side was seriously intent upon arriving at an agreement. On that basis, a compromise was reached that involved concessions by both sides.[24]

CHINESE ORGANISATIONAL PROBLEMS IN APPROACHING 1997

The new atmosphere of cooperation with Britain was still limited by the deep cultural divides, misunderstandings and distrust, but it was born of necessity within the context of the interests of the successors to Deng Xiaoping. Since Britain also seeks a smooth and graceful transition of sovereignty, there can be little doubt that the interests of both sides coincide perhaps as never before. But in the twilight of the British colonial era, the British dimension of the Hong Kong government is of declining significance and the key question has become one of China's relations with the people of Hong Kong.

Three key problems remain to be addressed include the future roles of the HKMAO and the NCNA, the place of the CCP in the HKSAR, and the ostracisation of the Hong Kong Democrats – the largest political party with the majority of votes cast by the electorate.

The HKMAO and the NCNA in Hong Kong, as we have seen, have notionally separate but overlapping responsibilities and there is a degree of rivalry between them as a result. The HKMAO officials have done more than 'carry out investigations and recommend policies', as one of its leading officials described its functions in July 1995.[25] They were active in organising the drafting and the consultations that led up to the making of the Basic Law. They have supplied personnel to China's negotiating teams in the Joint Liaison Group and elsewhere. They have been actively engaged in receiving visitors and delegations from Hong Kong and they have often pronounced on important policy matters, sometimes of a technical kind involving major infrastructure projects. In addition to its propaganda functions, the NCNA has served as the official representative of the Chinese government, and it has also been charged with winning over the support of most groups in the territory and isolating those identified as enemies (i.e. united front work). It has also been organised in many respects as a 'shadow government' not only within Hong Kong, but also in assisting in the conduct of China's relations with other Chinese communities in the region and hence with Southeast Asia as a whole.

These roles will have to be substantially modified, if not abolished altogether, by 1 July 1997. Otherwise, either separately or together, the HKMAO and the NCNA would become alternative centres of authority to the Chief Executive and his government of the SAR. Indeed, because of their links with Beijing, they would be seen to represent the wishes and demands of the Central Government and would be expected to prevail in the event of any differences with the Chief Executive. This would be a recipe for confusion and for the undermining of the rule of law. If the Chinese concept of 'one country two systems' as expressed in the Joint Declaration and the Basic Law is to have any credibility, the government of the HKSAR headed by its Chief Executive has got to be seen to be able to govern as an autonomous entity. It must not be seen to be subordinate to any organ of the Chinese Government other than that of the Central Government itself, and even in the Central Government it will be subject to carefully defined limits. One of the reasons that the NPC formally passed the Basic Law was to ensure that China's domestic organisations would also be subject to its provisions.[26]

If by 1 July 1997 the HKMAO and the NCNA were to be stripped of those functions that would challenge the authority of the incoming Chief Executive, interesting questions would arise about their exercise of those functions until then. As the key Chinese institutions responsible for completing the transition from British to Chinese (Hong Kong) administration, they would lack any institutional interest in its outcome. Moreover, just as the significance of Britain is declining within Hong Kong with the approach of the 1997 deadline, so presumably the significance of the HKMAO and the NCNA as centres of authority will ebb away once a Chief Executive designate is nominated and begins work in shaping the future government. As these two organisations constitute the main centres of China's expertise on Hong Kong's affairs, the Central Government will have to find ways of where best to deploy the relevant personnel, archives, files etc. Two obvious institutions where many could be relocated would be within the State Council and the National People's Congress as bodies to which the Chief Executive is accountable according to the Basic Law. According to the Basic Law, in dealing with Hong Kong questions the Standing Committee of the NPC will take advice from its Committee of the Basic Law of the HKSAR. But the NPC is not part of the executive branch concerned with the implementation of policy. Presumably, some of the expert personnel from the NCNA and the HKMAO could be attached to the office of the Ministry of Foreign Affairs that will be set up in Hong Kong in accordance with the Basic Law. At the time of writing (September 1995) there is not much evidence that the Chinese side has paid much attention to these potentially serious problems.[27]

The role of the Chinese Communist Party in the future HKSAR is also fraught with uncertainties. Ever since it was founded in 1948 by the late Qiao Guanhua (whose patron was Zhou Enlai and who became Foreign Minister until he fell in 1976 because of his association with the 'Gang of Four'), the NCNA has provided leadership for the CCP members in Hong Kong. The communists in Hong Kong, as represented in the NCNA, may be divided into three categories: the northerners who have been subject to tight Party discipline, who speak no Cantonese and are not very well attuned to the mores of Hong Kong; the so-called 'cradle communists', the locals whose parents were communists, or who went to communist schools or are employed by communists, who collectively are well attuned to Hong Kong but are said to lack true communist discipline; and, finally, the trade unionists and the ex-guerilla veterans who are tough, but less attuned to either reformed China or to contemporary Hong Kong. A defector has claimed that the NCNA has built up a network of communist cadres intended to rule Hong Kong after 1997.[28] Unless the NCNA has managed to have recruited surreptitiously a number of 'sleepers' among Hong Kong's senior civil service (which seems very unlikely), it is difficult to see how that could be done without once again undermining the authority of the government of the future HKSAR and its Chief Executive.

The future role and presence of the CCP in Hong Kong necessarily raises several questions of great importance that are unlikely to be answered in public. The CCP is unlikely to be set up openly as a political party in Hong Kong as it would inevitably be seen as the true locus of authority and, additionally, it would not wish to be placed in a position where it might be obliged to subject itself to the uncertainties of elections contested by secret ballot. It is possible that a reformed NCNA could continue to be the locus of authority for communist party members, but under these conditions the NCNA would have had to have been clearly disassociated from any of its 'shadowy' governmental functions. That would leave open the question of how the CCP would exercise effective supervision over the government of the HKSAR without, at the same time, being seen to undermine its authority. One way would be to take away from the CCP in Hong Kong the task of supervising the government of the SAR. The Chief Executive, for example, could be required, in effect, to consult with the head of the Ministry of Foreign Affairs Office to be located in Hong Kong. The Chief Executive could also be expected to appoint 'pro-China figures' to sit on the Executive Council, whom he/she is required to consult by the Basic Law.[29]

One course of action that might prove attractive to Beijing would be to provide the Chief Executive with an 'adviser' who would have access to all the confidential government papers on policy and personnel matters. If it were thought necessary to formalise the position, precedents exist within the current administrative arrangements for such personnel as the 'Political Adviser' or the head of the Central Policy Unit. China's leaders could be expected to require a senior communist to be placed at the heart of government with access to any information or papers, however secret, so that he would be in a position to liaise with the commander of the local People's Liberation Army in the event of an emergency. Only such a person could be relied upon to assess the situation correctly from Beijing's point of view and it would be essential for that person to be appraised of all the information at the disposal of the HKSAR government. In particular, it would be necessary to know as much as possible about the senior members of the civil service to determine from Beijing's point of view how reliable they would be in a crisis. To be truly effective, such a person should be discrete and entirely out of the public view.

COOPERATION WITH BRITAIN

By the terms of the Joint Declaration, consultation between Britain and China should intensify in the latter stages of the transition. As we have seen, agreements on the disposal of military lands and on the basis for financing the airport took place in the latter half of 1994 and, following a decision by the politburo in March 1995, a better atmosphere of cooperation emerged in June that year that was reflected in agreements on the Court of Final Appeal and on the final arrangements for raising the funds for the airport. Nevertheless, the considerable distrust that existed between the two sides has far from dissipated. The Chinese continue to be baffled by British claims to be exercising a moral responsibility on behalf of the people of Hong Kong and they continue to believe that the British key interest is to extract as much money from the territory as possible. Whenever it may become evident that Britain is not pursuing its commercial interests, ulterior motives are immediately suspected.

The Chinese side has continued to misunderstand Patten and has been unable to accept that in practice it is he who makes British policy on Hong Kong. In January 1995, a senior editor of the principal local communist paper, Ta Kung Pao, and one of the heads of the Institute for One Country Two Systems (located in the old Bank of China building), separately complained to the author of their failure to persuade Beijing to recognise that Patten played the key role in Britain's policy making over Hong Kong. Beijing was unable to accept that as a subordinate to the Prime Minister he could dictate policy on such an important issue. As one of them put it:

Beijing is used to a situation in which if the mayor of a major city is told to jump, the only question is how high.[30]

For its part, the British side continues to believe that China's leaders have an imperfect understanding of Hong Kong and how it works. The depth of the gulf between the two sides became evident from Beijing's dismissal of the September 1995 elections as 'irrelevant' and of its angry reaction to Patten's public proposal of 22 September to allow all 3.5 million British passport holders in Hong Kong the right of abode in Britain. What he saw as measure to reassure Hong Kong people and to give them the confidence to stay beyond the transfer of sovereignty, China's leaders saw as yet another scheme by the British to undermine the transfer of sovereignty by either encouraging pro-British people to stay on and exert influence on Britain's behalf or by facilitating their departure and so plunge the new HKSAR into turmoil. The Governor was accused by the Chinese side of seeking to change negotiated agreements ahead of the handover in 1997. A senior NCNA official added that the Governor's comments were not conducive to improving Sino-British relations in the lead-up to the visit to London of Vice Premier and Foreign Minister Qian Qichen that was due on 2–4 October. As it happened, the British government rejected the suggestion the following day. The British Labour Party also rejected it and its spokesman said that Patten's statement 'must raise doubts about his own confidence in the arrangements that he has put in place'.[31]

Even if this last controversy were to be overcome, the two sides would still have to grapple with the legacy of the 1992–1994 period of the breakdown in communications, the most important of which is the Chinese pledge to replace the three tiers of representative bodies elected under the 1992 Patten proposals. The critical one is the Legislative Council and the Chinese public commitment to set up on 1 July 1997 a provisional body to assume its functions and prepare for new elections on a different electoral system. The (British) Hong Kong government can hardly be expected in the transition period to cooperate in the preparations to dismantle what it considers to be the legitimate representative bodies chosen by the people of Hong Kong in open and free elections. That would contribute to undermining its own authority, questioning the rule of law, and even possibly making the territory ungovernable.

Even if the question of preparing for the provisional legislature could be set aside as exclusively a Chinese problem, it is nevertheless potentially a highly destabilising issue. It is possible that the Chinese side may be willing to listen to such advice as the British may wish to give on a confidential basis as to how the problem may be addressed so as to keep its destabilising implications to a minimum. But that would depend on how much good will has been established in the interim. Meanwhile, from the perspective of the British (Hong Kong) government there are many outstanding technical, but important, matters on which agreement is needed in the Joint Liaison Group to improve the chances of a successful transfer of sovereignty. These include questions about the right of abode, air services agreements, the localisation of laws etc. Clearly, good progress in these matters would show that a process of cooperation is possible despite the distrust and it could establish a basis for mutual confidence in addressing the more contentious matters.

In October 1994, Governor Patten pledged that his government would cooperate with the Preparatory Committee, the Chief Executive designate, future designated members of the Executive Council and Principal Officials of the future SAP. He also offered the full cooperation of the outgoing British Garrison in providing a smooth handover of defence responsibilities to the Chinese military authorities. Meanwhile, the Governor pointed out that in many areas there was already an impressive array of contacts and working relations between every part of the Hong Kong administration and their colleagues in China at both central and local levels. These included close cross border links on security, immigration, smuggling, trade, transport etc. Bilateral cooperation between regulatory authorities was responsible for the securities markets that reinforces the stability and integrity of the territory's financial system.[32]

On the positive side, it is also important to recognise the extent of the agreements that have been reached in the more than thirty plenary and hundreds of expert level meetings of the Joint Liaison Group. In addition to those of the airport and the Court of Final Appeal, there have been agreements on military lands; on common approaches to eight important franchises, contracts and licences which will continue beyond 1997, including those for the two power companies; on Hong Kong's continued participation in twenty-nine international organisations, including the GATT/WTO; on the continued application of 161 multilateral treaties; on localising fifty-six UK enactments covering such topics as aviation; and on nine investment promotion and protection agreements.[33]

Perhaps the most important development that has a bearing on the last phase of the transition is the growing set of interactions between the Hong Kong civil servants and Chinese government officials. These range from programmes by which senior Hong Kong officials spend up to three months in the prestigious Qinghua University learning about China's administrative practices to hundreds of arrangements for delegations of officials from China to visit Hong Kong for on-the-spot learning. In a vast variety of topics, officials of both sides contact each other directly and work together on matters that range from audit work to fire fighting. A truly significant breakthrough was the visit to Beijing by the Chief Secretary, Mrs Anson Chan, in July 1995 when she discussed with Vice Premier and Foreign Secretary, Qian Qichen, and with Director of HKMAO, Lu Ping, matters concerning the Hong Kong economy, the civil service and the transition. The improvement in Sino-British relations found practical expression in the agreement reached during Qian Qichen's visit to London in early October to establsh a liaison office in the Hong Kong government to facilitate cooperation with the Preparatory Committee. Nevertheless, the critical issue remains that of the provisional legislature. Much depends on whether Britain and China can sustain the new spirit of cooperation and on how the Legislative Council elected in September 1995 conducts itself. The Chinese side would be more likely to be persuaded to compromise if the Legislative Council should be seen as contributing to the process of government rather than obstructing the executive at every turn.

CHINESE APPROACHES TO HONG KONG IN THE TRANSITION TO 1997

Since 1992 the Chinese authorities may be said to have developed two separate but related approaches to preparing people in Hong Kong for the transition. The first has been to continue the long-standing attempt to cultivate support through building a united front; and the second has involved establishing a body of people who will constitute the trusted new political élite on whom the Chinese will draw in easing the transition and in providing local leadership beyond 1997. Both have been conducted through the HKMAO and the NCNA under the leadership of Lu Ping and Zhou Nan, respectively. In 1995 there were indications that the central leaders were dissatisfied with the united front work in particular. In his talk of 13 March 1995, to which reference has already been made, Li Ruihuan implicitly criticised the handling of Hong Kong affairs by acknowledging the leadership's ignorance of what made it work.[34] Privately, Chinese researchers claimed that Zhou Nan in particular had been criticised by senior military personnel and by some central leaders for being too reclusive and 'not doing a good job' in united front work.[35]

Whatever criticisms may be levelled at the HKMAO and the NCNA about their failings in winning over the 'hearts and minds' of people in Hong Kong, it should be appreciated that they have had to operate where the local people have time and again displayed a fundamental lack of trust and confidence in the Chinese Central Government itself. Surveys of public opinion in 1985 showed 42.9 per cent distrusted the Chinese government as compared to 31.5 per cent who trusted it. The figures for the Hong Kong government were 16.8 and 73.1 per cent, respectively. In February 1994, only 29 per cent were satisfied with the performance of the Chinese government in China as compared to 58 per cent who expressed satisfaction with the performance of the Hong Kong government.[36] These opinions were being expressed by a population that may be considered to be highly knowledgeable about public affairs. A local political scientist noted:

> No population of similar size on earth has so many daily news-papers: over twenty in Chinese and five in English . . . [according to surveys] nearly ninety per cent of Hong Kong people considered themselves informed to one degree or another about government policies related to their livelihood. . . . On Chinese affairs, over two-thirds considered themselves informed or had personal experience of Chinese realities.[37]

In the light of the poor view taken locally of the performance of the Chinese government, Chinese propaganda in Hong Kong may be said to have elicited a degree of success when fifty per cent of those surveyed in early 1994 expressed some degree of trust in the Chinese government to interpret the Basic Law in the best interest of the Hong Kong people as opposed to forty-two per cent who indicated no trust at all. However, only four per cent indicated a 'strong trust'.[38]

In June 1993, following its rejection of the Patten proposals for political reform as violations of previous agreements, the Chinese side set up the Preliminary Working Committee for the Preparatory Committee to be established according to the Basic Law in 1996. Fifty-seven members were appointed initially and another thirteen were added in May 1994. Thirty-seven of these come from Hong Kong and they constitute in the words of the liberal Legislative Councillor, Christine Loh, 'an odd assortment of long-time leftists, mixed with recent converts... '.[39] The PWC is headed by Vice Premier and Foreign Minister, Qian Qichen, and it has been presented as part of China's 'second stove' or alternative authority to that of the (British) Hong Kong government. Less controversially, Beijing has described it as 'laying the foundation' for the transfer of sovereignty. The PWC is made up of several sub-groups that carry out investigations and offer recommendations and public advice that Beijing has chosen to highlight. Beijing has treated the PWC as an important body, as can be seen from the fact the Executive Deputy Chief of the General Staff of the People's Liberation Army, Xu Huizi, was a member and represented the military's involvement in Hong Kong affairs.[40] At times, its members have embarrassed Beijing by ill-considered proposals such as suggesting that school textbooks be screened for political correctness *vis-à-vis* China, or recommending that Hong Kong Chinese should lose the automatic right to live in Hong Kong if they acquired foreign passports. But more damaging for Beijing is that, in a survey taken in early 1995, sixty-five per cent considered that the PWC did not work for the interests of Hong Kong.[41]

In 1992, the Chinese authorities appointed forty-four people as the first group of advisers on Hong Kong affairs. By early 1995, more than 700 had been chosen by name. They were drawn from Hong Kong's élite to include people from business, the professions, the universities, former civil servants, former drafters and consultants on the Basic Law, (pro-China) trade unions and representatives on mainland institutions. They have been described as in the main 'pro-business figures willing to support any government that can ensure political stability and economic freedom'.[42] Typically, the terms of reference and precise functions of these advisers were left open and ill-defined. As one who held an appointment briefly explained, the role of adviser entails

> no officially stated functions, although whenever Chinese officials talk about Hong Kong affairs advisers, they always emphasise that they will help with the transition. But there was never any terms of reference as to what exactly we would do.[43]

The most important point about these advisers is perhaps the deliberate exclusion of all members of the Democratic Party led by Martin Lee. Anthony Cheung, the chairman of Meeting Point, had his appointment as 'adviser' withdrawn within a month because of his party's merger with the United Democrats to form the Democratic

Party. This is the political party that has consistently won the majority of seats in all the openly-contested direct popular elections in Hong Kong. The deliberate exclusion and the attempt by 'pro-China' people to stigmatise the Democrats as 'pro-British' may be seen as an attempt to intimidate its supporters and to discourage waverers from associating themselves with the party. It is possible that these tactics may have prevented the Democrats from enjoying even greater support, but they can hardly be described as a success if they cause the Chinese authorities to be seen to be pitted against the most widely supported political party in Hong Kong. After all, classical CCP united front strategy called for defining the axis of conflict so as to exclude at any stage only a minority (5–10 per cent) as the enemy to be ostracised. The task of the CCP strategists was to exploit divisions among opponents, win over the waverers and consolidate their position of their reliable supporters ensuring all the time that they could claim overwhelming majority support. Whatever else may be said about China's united front strategy in Hong Kong, it cannot be claimed to correspond with the classic requirements.

Meanwhile, the polarisation of Hong Kong has continued apace. Those in the public arena have been labelled as either 'pro-China' or 'pro-British'. It has heightened tensions and anxieties in the territory. In the universities, for example, where decisions about promotion and the allocation of resources are difficult at the best of times, the atmosphere has been poisoned, especially in social science faculties in the 'new' universities. Trust, which is necessary for the proper conduct of the professions, has diminished as distinctions have been drawn between those who have, or do not have, foreign passports. It is more difficult to take up public positions on issues without being accused of acting in bad faith or pursuing private gain. Amid this general atmosphere of fear and suspicion, PWC members are regularly perceived, rightly or wrongly, as seeking to ingratiate themselves with Beijing. Under such conditions it has become very difficult for political figures within Hong Kong to take the initiative to establish contact with leaders in Beijing, even at a time when there are good reasons to think that they, like Li Ruihuan, may be receptive to beginning new dialogues.

Senior members of the HKMAO in Beijing have conceded that a polarisation has taken place in Hong Kong. They traced its origins back to the ramifications of the Tiananmen events of the Spring and early Summer of 1989. They argued that the British government misjudged the situation and ceased to cooperate with China in solving difficulties as had been the case in the period since 1984 now called 'the honeymoon years'. But since 1989, in their view, divergences grew and these led to the polarisation. It was at this time that political parties emerged in Hong Kong where they had not existed in the previous 150 years of British rule. The earliest and biggest grew out of the 1989 'anti-China' All Hong Kong Alliance in Support of the Chinese Patriotic Pro-Democracy Movement, which became the Democratic Party under the leadership of Martin Lee. But other parties also emerged. Another reason was the British decision to allocate 50,000 passports. 'This too led to division [in Hong Kong].' However, the main concern of the HKMAO officials was what they regarded as the politicisation of Hong Kong. They explained that they did not want it to become what they called 'a political city'. When pressed to explain their specific concerns, they said they feared the emergence of many quarrelling parties who would prevent the passing of government bills in the Legislative Council. That would diminish the effectiveness of government and cause foreign investors to doubt the territory's political stability. Hong Kong would then cease to be an international financial centre. They argued that the main success of the British was in establishing an executive-led government that was coordinated with the legislature and to a certain extent restrained by it, but not obstructed by it.[44]

Clearly, from Beijing's perspective, much depends on the performance of the Legislative Council elected in September 1995. Although the understanding of the democratic political process shown by the HKMAO officials may be seriously faulted, there is still time for them to recognise the constructive role that the Legislative Council plays in the Hong Kong system of government.[45] But it is difficult to see how Beijing can expect to retain the confidence, especially of the professional middle classes (many of whom do have the option of leaving) if it is to continue to refuse to have any dealings with the members of the Democratic Party. Not only have more people voted for it than any other party, but it also espouses the liberal principles which are the foundation for the proper conduct of professional life and for freedom under the law which has made Hong Kong a tolerable place to live, work and prosper for the overwhelming majority of its people.

Chapter 5

1997 and beyond

Any assessment of the consequences and implications of the Chinese recovery of Hong Kong must necessarily be speculative at this stage. However, on the assumptions that Chinese politics will not be subject to some unexpected upheaval and that sovereignty will be transferred without major problems, it is possible to identify many of the key issues that will arise and to suggest how they may be dealt with. These may be best considered by discussing separately the perspectives and interests of the Chinese and Hong Kong sides. The international dimensions of the takeover must also be addressed before attempting to bring the different strands together.

THE IMPLICATIONS FOR CHINA

Over the years since Deng Xiaoping first indicated in his talk with Governor MacLehose in 1979 that the Chinese government intended to allow Hong Kong to continue as a capitalist enclave after the resumption of sovereignty, the Chinese side has gone a long way in developing its ideas as to how this would be done. The agreement with Britain in 1984 and the enactment of the Basic Law have spelt out, in considerable detail, the various dimensions of Hong Kong's way of life that are to be preserved and the system of government by which the projected 'high degree of autonomy' is to be exercised. Nevertheless, considerable uncertainties remain about the extent of autonomy that will be allowed in practice. The Chinese side will be particularly concerned by its failure to have built extensive public support, as shown by the results of the September 1995 elections. Whatever Beijing may decide to do with its provisional legislature, the lack of significant public support will probably cause Beijing to take an even closer interest in the affairs of Hong Kong after the transfer of sovereignty.

However, a big question mark hangs over the transfer of sovereignty because of the Chinese pledge to replace the Legislative Council elected in September 1995 with a provisional body of nominated members. By deviating from the expressed wishes of Hong Kong's voters, the Chinese side risks undermining the credibility of the new body and the Chinese authorities will have to weigh carefully the possibility of undermining public confidence in Hong Kong itself. The destabilising implications of the nomination of a provisional legislature presumably will become evident to the Chinese authorities as the due date draws near. Meanwhile, they have not revealed their precise intentions and the analysis below is based on the assumption that China's leaders will find a way of proceeding without falling at this first hurdle.

Meanwhile, by the time of writing in September 1995, China's leaders have identified a number of concerns that will cause them to be closely involved in Hong Kong affairs even after 1997. These include matters to do with sovereignty; patriotism; subversion; undue haste in developing democracy; transforming Hong Kong into a 'political city'; 'internationalising' Hong Kong; preventing its capitalist character from being undermined by 'welfarism'; and ensuring that a proper balance is kept between the central government in Beijing and the local government of Hong Kong. Taken together, these concerns will mean that Beijing will be much more closely involved in the running of Hong Kong than London ever was.

Perhaps few issues figure more largely than the question of sovereignty. An official explanation of the conduct of the negotiations with Britain published in October 1993 under the auspices of the Central Committee of the CCP claimed that, even in the period of the negotiations that led to the Sino-British agreement in 1984, British proposals were 'designed to turn Hong Kong into an independent or semi-independent political entity subject to Britain's influence'.[1] This fundamental distrust was evident throughout the subsequent course of the negotiations during the thirteen years leading up to 1997. It was sharply re-emphasised in the wake of Tiananmen in 1989 and again in 1992–1993 after Governor Patten put forward his proposals for electoral reform. In 1995, a better spirit of cooperation emerged between the two sides and it remains to be seen whether that can be continued up to and beyond 1997. Part of the problem has been that the British side has tended to underestimate the significance of the question of sovereignty in Chinese approaches to the Hong Kong issue. However, the key issue that the Chinese authorities will have to address is how to balance their passion for asserting sovereignty with their interest in maintaining stability in Hong Kong. Too strong an assertion of the former could result in frightening Hong Kong's middle-class professionals into leaving the territory in droves with calamitous consequences for the HKSAR.

THE SOVEREIGNTY AND PATRIOTIC DIMENSIONS

The argument that the Chinese authorities will be very concerned to allow as much continuity in Hong Kong because of its great economic importance fails to take into account the importance of politics and, in particular, the significance of the nationalist dimensions that have acquired special salience at this time of political succession to Deng Xiaoping.

The restoration of Chinese sovereignty on 1 July 1997 has been presented by China's leaders as a momentous event in the modern history of their country. It is occurring at a time in which the patriotic or nationalistic sentiment is being emphasised as perhaps the only viable ideology around which to unite the country. The agreement to recover Hong Kong has long been seen as one of Deng Xiaoping's major achievements. Indeed, China's leaders have raised the significance attached to the occasion as the due date has drawn closer. With the publication of the third volume of Deng Xiaoping's *Selected Works* in October 1993, the official Chinese account of Deng Xiaoping's talk to Mrs Thatcher on their first meeting on 24 September 1982 was released for the first time. It was significantly titled 'Our Basic Position On the Question of Hong Kong', and it records him as making the following very remarkable statements:

> On the question of sovereignty, China has no room for man-oeuvre.... If China failed to recover Hong Kong in 1997, when the People's Republic will have been established for 48 years, no Chinese leaders or government would be able to justify themselves for that failure before the Chinese people or before the people of the world. It would mean that the present Chinese government was just like the government of the late Qing Dynasty and that the present Chinese leaders were just like Li Hongzhang![2] ...
>
> If we failed to recover Hong Kong in 15 years the people would no longer have reason to trust us, and any Chinese government

would have no alternative but to step down and voluntarily leave the political arena.[3]

Aimed primarily at the domestic audience in China and in Hong Kong too, these statements both reflect and promote a strong sense of nationalism. Interestingly, this particular talk was left out from the previous collection of Deng Xiaoping's talks and writings of the period 1982–1987 published in 1987 under the title *Fundamental Issues in Present Day China*, even though it included all the others in the period 1982–1984.[4] Since this 1982 talk was officially published in an authorised version only in 1993, it should be understood as reflecting the situation back then. It carries special weight in view of the pending political succession. A domestic political élite accustomed to reading official texts for any new nuances or hidden meanings could hardly have failed to note the pointed reference to the consequences of failure for '*any* Chinese government' (emphasis added). Deng's successors may be seen as having prepared the ground for bolstering their prestige as a result of presiding over the formal recovery of Hong Kong.

The talk and the late date of its publication is a sharp reminder, if one were needed, that the politics of sovereignty and national reunification override everything else, including economics. This dovetails in with the increased nationalistic tone of many of Beijing's pronouncements in the 1990s. The response of leaders to the Tiananmen events and the demise of communist rule in Eastern Europe and the collapse of the Soviet Union linked the survival of the CCP with the promotion of a patriotic theme that stressed authoritarian leadership, stability and, above all, the provision of prosperity. The latter was seen as the key for retaining popular support and avoiding another Tiananmen incident, but it required the further expansion of the operations of the market and increasing the openness to the outside world. The more conservative leaders tried to use the patriotic theme as a reason to restrict contacts with the West and to constrain the development of market forces. They argued that these were sources of 'spiritual pollution' and were part of the American campaign to undermine the Chinese system by the policy of 'peaceful evolution'. Indeed, Deng Xiaoping himself had to intervene at times to prevent the nationalistic impulses from being hijacked by others to obstruct his policies on the open door and on maintaining workable relations with the USA.[5] Jiang Zemin's speeches during this period have repeatedly stressed nationalist themes and he was associated with a campaign to inculcate 'Patriotic Education' launched in September 1994. More broadly, the nationalist theme has found a ready response in a population for whom communist ideology has become largely irrelevant, but whose view of the post-communist disorders in Russia in particular has tarnished the appeal of the alleged Western democratic alternative.[6]

The nationalist mood is likely to prevail for some time as it serves the interests of the new collective leadership and, paradoxically, the more centrifugal forces who do not wish to appear as destroyers of national unity.[7] It also serves the interests of society as a whole.

A period of relative political stability and intellectual stagnation has combined with economic frenzy to create the possibility for a rough-and-ready confluence of interests under the umbrella of patriotism.[8]

Under these conditions, especially when coupled with the deep suspicions of British designs to retain influence (which were intensified by the conflict with Governor Chris Patten), Beijing can be expected to monitor very closely the performance of the new HKSAR to ensure that its understanding of sovereignty is not breached. Since the Chinese view of sovereignty is more inclusive and absolutist than that which generally prevails in the contemporary West, the Chinese authorities are likely to be acutely sensitive on the issue.[9]

Beijing's attachment to what it terms 'patriotism' will also cause it to be directly involved in the affairs of the HKSAR, especially in determining whether people are qualified to hold political office. Beijing will have to balance its desire for stability with its concern for political loyalty in confirming senior appointments in the civil service. Even before Patten introduced his controversial proposals, the Chinese in the Basic Law had insisted that all members of the legislature would have to be tested for their 'patriotism' before they would be allowed to serve in the legislature of the HKSAR. This highly political term lacks precise legal definition and, like most key concepts put forward by Beijing's leaders, the practical meaning and application of 'patriotism' depends upon the political context of the day. As was discussed in Chapter 4, the question of the alleged patriotism of politicians and others in Hong Kong has distorted Beijing's traditional approach to building a united front.

SUBVERSION AND THE DEMOCRACY QUESTION

China's paramount leader, Deng Xiaoping, made known his concerns about these issues well before the Tiananmen crisis of 1989. Consider, for example, the unequivocal statement by Deng Xiaoping to drafters of the Basic Law in 1987 that was published authoritatively for the first time in October 1993 in Volume III of his selected works:

> Don't ever think that everything would be all right if Hong Kong affairs were administered solely by Hong Kong people while the Central Government had nothing to do with the matter. That simply wouldn't work – it's not a realistic idea. The Central Government certainly will not intervene in the day-to-day affairs of the special administrative region, nor is that necessary. But isn't it possible that something could happen in the region that might jeopardize the fundamental interests of the country? . . .
>
> You should also consider a few other things. For example, after 1997 we shall still allow people in Hong Kong to attack the Chinese Communist Party and China verbally, but what if they should turn their words into action, trying to convert Hong Kong into a base of opposition to the mainland under the pretext of 'democracy'? Then we should have no choice but to intervene . . . [10]

Deng had earlier poured scorn on Western democracy denying that it was applicable to China and questioning whether it would be good for Hong Kong. He queried whether a general election would necessarily bring out people 'who love the motherland and Hong Kong. . . . Even if a general election were to be held, there would have to be a transition period, and preparations for the election would have to be made step by step'.[11]

The Basic Law in the end opted for a gradual approach so that the 60-member legislature would begin with 20 members directly elected, rising to 24 and then to 30 (or half), leaving it open for further changes from the year 2007. That would also be the year in which it would be possible to choose the Chief Executive by direct elections. Meanwhile, in response to the Patten electoral reforms, the Chinese authorities have pledged to replace the 1995 elected Legislative Council with a provisional one whose task in its first year will be to devise a new system of elections. The Chinese side has once again shown that its political priorities override any economic uncertainties that such a potentially disruptive move may bring about. Yet the Chinese reaction to the September 1995 elections of the Legislative Council displayed a degree of ambivalence. Rather than boycott them altogether, the Chinese side openly supported the political party and the candidates they deemed sympathetic, only to issue a public attack upon the elections on the actual day of the polls. Once again, the Chinese repeated their pledge to replace the elected body upon their resumption of sovereignty. Meanwhile, they attacked the Democratic Party as hostile to China. Indeed, the leaders of the Democratic Party, Szeto Wah and Martin Lee, have been singled out as subversives since the crisis of 4 June 1989. In particular, Beijing objected to the Hong Kong Alliance in support of the Patriotic Democratic Movement in China – an umbrella group that raised money for the demonstrators in Beijing and that helped the escape of prominent leaders of the movement. What may have particularly disturbed Beijing was the extensive support that the Alliance had enjoyed in Hong Kong. Two CCP-controlled trade unions left the Alliance only days before it was declared to be 'counter-revolutionary' and the Hong Kong Federation of Students had to be warned by the NCNA before it too quit the Alliance. Beijing was reported to have asked the Hong Kong government to ban the Alliance, but this was refused.[12] This was at the height of Beijing's fears of Western attempts to undermine communism in China by a strategy of peaceful evolution. The clause in the Basic Law against subversion that had been published in the earlier drafts of April 1988 and February 1989 was tightened and enlarged in the final version that was approved by the National People's Congress in April 1990.

Having little understanding or experience of democracy, Beijing's leaders suspect it greatly and have, so far, not been persuaded to find ways to accommodate the Democratic Party because it has consistently garnered the largest number of votes and seats in the Legislative Council. On the contrary, Chinese suspicions seem to have been raised further by the relative electoral success of the Democrats. They have at times explained this away by claiming that the British deliberately chose an electoral system that favoured the Democrats and penalised those more sympathetic to Chinese interests.[13] The fact that the Democrats opposed the Patten proposals on the grounds that they did not extend the franchise still further to make all 60 seats directly elected from geographical constituencies would have condemned them further in Chinese eyes. The argument often made by Democrats that the future viability of Hong Kong depends upon the development of political reform in China has served to confirm China's leaders in the inherently subversive character of the Democrats.

Beijing's commitment to nominate a provisional legislature obviously provides it with many opportunities to intervene in the affairs of the HKSAR. But the Chinese authorities may be well advised to attempt to bridge the vast gulf that exists between them and the Democrats who time and again have been shown to be supported by a large majority of Hong Kong's voters. Official Chinese commentaries have complained that the electoral system chosen by Governor Patten unfairly favoured 'pro-British' candidates. But any examination of the scale of the victory of the Democrats and of the defeat of the candidates favoured by NCNA would suggest that the results would not have been reversed by following a different electoral system. The Chinese authorities are said to have considered introducing a system of multi-seat constituencies, such as in Japan, or a system of proportional representation, as in some West-European countries (and more recently in New Zealand). But provided that they were conducted fairly, elections under any other system would not have denied victory to the Democrats. At most, a different system may have affected the precise distribution of seats in the legislature but, short of deliberate and unfair manipulation, it would not have been able magically to reverse the verdict and leave the Democrats in the minority of the directly-elected seats. Beijing cannot look to the electoral system to save it from the awkward problem that the majority of the people in Hong Kong support a party whose leaders it regards as subversive and unpatriotic.

POLITICISATION AND INTERNATIONALISATION

As discussed in Chapter 4, Beijing objects to the transformation of Hong Kong into a 'political city'. The term refers to the possibility that the Legislative Council might become too fractured by party politics to allow the Executive to govern effectively. The passage of important bills and legislation could be obstructed. Deng Xiaoping himself prepared the ground for intervention under such circumstances:

> Isn't it possible that something could happen there that would jeopardize the fundamental interests of Hong Kong itself? Can anyone imagine that there are no forces that might engage in obstruction or sabotage?... If the Central Government were to abandon all its power, there might be turmoil that would damage Hong Kong's interests. *Therefore it is to Hong Kong's advantage,*

not its disadvantage, for the Central Government to retain some power there.[14]

(Emphasis added)

In the same speech of April 1987, Deng went on to suggest to the drafters of the Basic Law that they should consider the following:

> After 1997 we shall still allow Hong Kong people to criticize the Chinese Communist Party and China, but what if they should turn their words into action, trying to convert Hong Kong into a base of opposition to the mainland under the pretext of 'democracy'? Then we would have no choice but to intervene; mainland troops stationed there would not necessarily be used. They would be used only if there were disturbances, serious disturbances. Anyway, intervention of some sort would be necessary![15]

In the event, the Basic Law did not directly address the issue, but some of the wording was sufficiently vague as to allow the Central Government 'to issue an order applying the relevant national laws in the Region'. One such occasion would arise if Beijing were to decide that there was 'turmoil within the HKSAR which endangers national unity or security [that] is beyond the control of the government of the region [and] that the Region is in a state of emergency' (Article 18). It should be noted that as in other instances the crucial word (in this case) 'turmoil', like 'patriotic' earlier, is not defined in legal terms.

Beijing has additionally warned against the 'internationalisation' of the city. This ill-defined term is what Beijing considers to be external interference in its sovereign domain. The Chinese authorities have raised no objection to Hong Kong's activities as an international entity especially in economic matters. Indeed, it is with China's backing that Hong Kong is a signatory to many international agreements and is a member of many international organisations. The ire of Beijing has been directed against what it perceives as attempts by others to weaken its domestic authority, undermine its sovereign claims or generally interfere in its attempts to re-establish unity with Hong Kong and Taiwan.

To this end, it has denounced any British assertions of a continued responsibility in the HKSAR and has particularly rejected the right of the US government to pronounce on its policies in Hong Kong as required by a Congressional Bill of 1992.[16] It has also reacted adversely to publicly-declared claims of other governments to pronounce on Hong Kong affairs because, like Canada or Australia, a large number of people from Hong Kong have recently established residence there and still maintain close ties with the territory.[17] But it has recognised that other countries do have interests in Hong Kong stemming from the period of British rule and that are expressed in accordance with the Joint Declaration and the Basic Law. For example, it is agreed that, subject to Chinese agreement, consulates could be maintained in the HKSAR even if the relevant states did not enjoy formal diplomatic relations with Beijing. The Chinese authorities have also allowed, in practice, that other kinds of external parties may be represented in Hong Kong provided that the relevant countries keep Beijing informed and do so in a way that does not embarrass the PRC, and/or that their presence should accord with Beijing's interests. For example, Beijing and Taipei found a way to establish unofficial representation by Taipei in Hong Kong through the offices of the Kuanghwa Travel Agency. Recognising the sensitivities of Beijing, the official Hong Kong yearbooks have refrained from any discussion of the high-profile foreign visits of Governors Wilson and Patten or, indeed, of distinguished foreign visits to Hong Kong. The yearbooks have confined themselves to publishing without comment photographs of the meetings of the governors with the foreign VIPs.

The Chinese side has not only been alert to alleged infringements of Chinese sovereignty over Hong Kong by foreign governments, but it has also taken steps to limit the foreign political links of Hong Kong people. Article 23 of the Basic Law that deals with subversion specifically requires the HKSAR to enact laws

> to prohibit foreign organizations or bodies from conducting political activities in the Region, and to prohibit political organizations or bodies of the Region from establishing ties with foreign political organizations or bodies.

It is unclear, for example, what implications this may have for Taiwanese organisations operating in Hong Kong, or whether elected Hong Kong representatives would be subject to limits on foreign travel (including Taiwan), or in meeting foreigners. Needless to say, no legal definitions are provided for the key terms. Would Article 23 also apply to human rights organisations, or to bodies concerned with the implementation of law? Elsewhere (Article 141), religious organisations and believers are permitted to maintain and develop relations with others of their ilk in other countries. Should the two provisions conflict it is believed that Article 23 would prevail.[18] Similar considerations apply to Article 149 which allows for a wide variety of non-governmental organisations in education, science, culture, sports, the professions etc. to maintain and develop relations with foreign counterparts.

In keeping with Chinese interests in facilitating the continuance of Hong Kong as an international economic and financial centre, the Basic Law allows the HKSAR to maintain and develop a wide range of international links and agreements with foreign governments and international organisations. Similarly, the HKSAR under the name of 'Hong Kong, China' is allowed to participate in international organisations and conferences not limited to states. For example, Hong Kong is a member of the Asia Pacific Economic Cooperation forum which allows membership by non-states even though it regularly discusses political questions as part of the informal summitry begun by President Clinton at the Seattle meeting in November 1993. The PRC also undertook to ensure that the HKSAR could maintain its separate status where it participates independently in organisations, whether or not the PRC is also a member. For example, unlike China, Hong Kong is a member of the World Trade Organization (the successor to the GATT). It is in keeping with the Joint Declaration that the PRC is committed to maintaining Hong Kong's separate international status.

The PRC stands to gain from its close association with Hong Kong's international links. Questions may be asked as to whether Beijing may take advantage of the situation to blur the differences with the HKSAR in order to benefit from its international commercial agreements as, for example, from its membership of the World Trade Organization from which the PRC is still excluded. In the long run, however, such 'cheating' would be self defeating. But this recognition of the Region's international standing obfuscates Beijing's opposition to what elsewhere it has described as 'internationalisation'. Since Hong Kong's international status is an important part of the territory's distinctive character and identity, the international community can contribute to the preservation of that identity by seeking to ensure that its international dimensions are not infringed. Moreover, governments of states whose companies have invested heavily in Hong Kong and who have thousands of citizens working there can be expected to remind Beijing that their interests would also be damaged by untoward events in the Region. 'Internationalisation' will probably remain a sore issue for Beijing for some time to come.

'WELFARISM'

Beijing's concern to maintain the capitalist system in Hong Kong has extended to opposing the introduction of further social welfare schemes. In part, this may be seen as a response to business concerns that the introduction of greater democracy will lead to demands for higher spending on welfare which, in turn, would result in higher taxes and in reducing Hong Kong's comparative advantage. But it can also be seen as linked to Chinese suspicions of British intentions. New welfare initiatives by the Hong Kong government are not seen as useful measures to improve the living conditions of the majority of the less affluent people of Hong Kong that can be met from the vast revenue surpluses. They tend to be perceived as part of a British scheme to denude the Hong Kong treasury of money and to leave the Region in disarray with mounting debts.[19] Consequently, this too is seen as a matter in which the Central Government may intervene.

The September 1995 elections introduced a new complexity for the Chinese authorities. The candidates that they supported, principally within the Democratic Alliance for the Betterment of Hong Kong (DAB), like the Democrats with whom they competed for the popular vote, also made demands for higher spending on welfare. That opens the prospect of the members of the two parties joining together in the Legislative Council to vote in favour of 'welfarism'. Together they would command a clear majority and, although the legislature lacks the constitutional powers to compel the executive to accept its bills especially where further governmental expenditure is required, the executive cannot govern without getting its own bills adopted. The British Hong Kong government could be embarrassed in the short run, but in the longer term this could become a serious problem for Beijing that could well strengthen its interventionist tendencies.

RELATIONS WITH THE CENTRAL GOVERNMENT

The provisions of the Basic Law ensure that in the event of any disagreement between the Central Government and the HKSAR it is the former that will prevail. It alone through the NPC possesses the authority to interpret and amend the Basic Law and has the right to review all legislation of the Region to determine its conformity with the Basic Law. Any bill deemed to contravene it with respect to the affairs of the Central Government or the relationship between the central authorities and the Region can be annulled and returned to the

Chief Executive for appropriate amendment. In order to avoid such a potentially demeaning and disruptive event, the Chief Executive is likely to cooperate closely with the members of the appropriate committee of the Standing Committee of the National People's Congress, which exercises final authority over these matters.

THE CONSTRAINTS ON INTERVENTION

Even though many political considerations may impel Beijing to intervene in the affairs of the HKSAR, these have to be weighed against other political goals and interests that militate against undue interference. Earlier, it was suggested that questions of sovereignty and political survival will outweigh economic interests and that it would be unwise to rely upon the Region's economic significance to guarantee the continuity in Hong Kong. But, since continued communist rule in China has been said to depend on maintaining high economic growth rates and continuing prosperity, economics itself has acquired a deep political significance in its own right. Since Hong Kong has played an important role in the rapid growth of the Chinese economy, China's leaders would pause long and hard before knowingly damaging its ability to continue in that vein.

Benign treatment cannot be taken for granted. China's new leaders are subject to contradictory impulses and pressures. In addition to the issues of national prestige involved in its recovery, Hong Kong is seen, on the one hand, as a source for enhancing the national economy and, hence, the political authority of the ruling communist party but, on the other hand, it is also seen as an instigator of national disintegration by being an exemplar of Western cultural and political norms. Even its economic role raises problems for the Chinese side for, although it serves the Chinese economy as a whole, Hong Kong's impact on Guangdong Province and to a lesser extent the other southern coastal provinces is so overwhelming as to lead to the description 'Greater Hong Kong'. The issue is not one of separatism, but rather one that arises out of the 'bring[ing] together [of] different parts of the Chinese world to their mutual benefit'.[20] The current themes of official patriotism make a special point of appealing to 'Chinese people' (*Huaren*) wherever they may be. That is to say, they include those who may be culturally or racially Chinese of different nationalities.[21] In other words, although Hong Kong may be seen as contributing to the clash of interests between the interior and coastal provinces, the real challenge is that of the introduction of diversity and a degree of pluralism into the hitherto supposedly unitary Chinese system.

As discussed in Chapter 4, the new leadership has additional incentives to be seen to succeed in effecting a smooth transfer of sovereignty. The Chinese authorities cannot be seen to be intolerant of allowing Hong Kong to practise the capitalist system with its rule of law and the numerous freedoms of its way of life as adumbrated in the Joint Declaration with Britain. If the formula of 'one country two systems' could not be applied to Hong Kong, where China can bring overwhelming power and influence to bear, the formula would be drained of any credibility as far as Taiwan was concerned. There would no longer be anything left of Beijing's policy for re-establishing unity with Taiwan on a peaceful basis. That would leave force as the only credible option. All the worst fears of China's neighbours and potential partners in the Asia-Pacific would be confirmed. Relations with the USA and Japan – the two countries of the greatest significance for China – would be damaged with consequences that would be difficult to calculate in advance. The costs to Beijing would be severe and as Beijing took on a more truculent position its neighbours and Taiwan could well succeed in finding countervailing power to balance against China. Economic development would suffer and a more isolated regime could very well acquire more neo-fascist characteristics.[22]

Despite their distrust of Britain and their suspicions about Hong Kong's Democratic Party and its leaders, China's new leaders will have powerful incentives to resist those nationalistic pressures that seek to rein in Hong Kong. The costs of riding roughshod over the Hong Kong 'way of life' (to cite the distinctive phrase of the Joint Declaration) should be sufficiently high as to sideline the voices of the centralists and conservatives (the 'Browns') whose interests and traditional ideological prejudices impel them to seek to establish controls over Hong Kong and its allegedly malevolent influence on the mainland. Nevertheless, the uncertainties of politics in Beijing where bargaining among competing bureaucratic interests will be linked to the jockeying for succession among the members of the collective leadership may result in policies that, from a broader perspective, would be deemed irrational. Policy making without a 'strong man', such as Mao Zedong or Deng Xiaoping, would be a new and uncertain experience for China.[23] The way the new leaders will handle the challenge of Hong Kong will provide a visible test as to their competence and self-confidence, which will have enormous consequences both at home and abroad.

THE IMPLICATIONS FOR HONG KONG

Much will depend upon the circumstances of the transfer of sovereignty. The situation would be eased if China and Britain had been able to cooperate sufficiently to settle the outstanding agenda in the Joint Liaison Group including the remaining air services agreements, the localisation of laws and the conditions of residence of people born in Hong Kong who sought to return after having established the right of residence abroad. A good working relationship with Britain would also assist the Chinese side in overcoming such problems as may be encountered in the immediate aftermath of the transfer of sovereignty. Similarly, the transfer would be greatly eased if the Chinese side had developed extensive institutionalised patterns of cooperation with Hong Kong's civil service. Much would also depend on the quality of the Chief Executive and the top civil servants – all of whose appointments will have been confirmed by Beijing. By that stage the Chief Executive and his staff should have familiarised themselves with the tasks and instruments of governing Hong Kong.

A great deal will depend upon the all important issue of confidence. That is to say, the confidence of Hong Kong people in the capacity of the HKSAR to provide good governance under the new sovereign power and the confidence of the local and foreign business communities in its ability to provide conditions in which the economy could operate as before. Accordingly, it would be to the advantage of the Region if the summer of 1997 were to coincide with a period in which the Chinese economy was experiencing an upswing in its recurring cycles of boom and retrenchment.

That would have an important bearing upon the judgement of the business people on whom Beijing seems to rely for the continued development of Hong Kong as a commercial and financial centre. The major international companies that operate in Hong Kong could easily transfer their personnel elsewhere, as was demonstrated when they cut back their representation when the cost of property became prohibitive in 1993/94.[24] Most multinational corporations have been careful to limit their investments in Hong Kong to a small proportion of their overall international investments and could readily transfer the investment elsewhere if the risk seemed prohibitive or the profits unattractive. The overwhelming majority of Hong Kong's business people have foreign passports and a large number of the important local firms have established a right to foreign domicile. They have spread their investments abroad for economic as well as political reasons and, under modern conditions, they could easily transfer their capital out of Hong Kong in the knowledge that if they so chose they could transfer it back just as easily and as quickly.

> In sum, the local and foreign business community in Hong Kong is well protected *vis-à-vis* uncertainty concerning the future of the territory. They have calculated their risks too.[25]

The middle-class professionals, who (to judge from the high proportion selected as advisers) have also been cultivated by Beijing, are perhaps not so readily mobile as the business people. Consequently, many have chosen to establish foreign residence abroad through emigration. More than half a million people have emigrated since 1981 and, although no figures have been kept about their occupations, the majority are thought to be middle-class professionals and their families. However, as noted in Chapter 4, the Hong Kong government estimates that at least twelve per cent of those who emigrated in the ten years before 1992 have returned. These are largely professional people who have left their families behind so that they can earn more money in the more congenial working environment of Hong Kong. These people could easily leave and senior government officials privately estimate that more than a million people currently resident in Hong Kong could leave at any time of their choice.[26] The remaining 4.5–5 million of the ordinary people in Hong Kong have no alternative but to stay and adapt as best they can.

At least five main issues will be significant in determining the immediate future of the HKSAR from the perspective of the business and middle-class professionals of Hong Kong whom many (including Beijing) see as the backbone of its economy. These may be listed as follows:

- What will be the future of the three tiers of representative institutions of government that Beijing has pledged to abolish?
- How will the Chief Executive relate to the Chinese Central Government and what will be the role of the all important Chinese Communist Party?

- Will the judiciary and the civil service be capable of resisting the corrosive intrusion of egregious corruption from the Chinese mainland?
- Will the professions be willing and able to uphold their independence against the twin threats of self censorship and pressure from Chinese authorities?
- Will the HKSAR be able to uphold successfully Hong Kong's distinctive international identity?

The provisional representative bodies

The Chinese government has publicly and repeatedly pledged to replace all three tiers of representative bodies elected under the proposals of Governor Chris Patten. These include the District Boards, the Regional and Urban Councils and the all-important Legislative Council. Beijing has argued that Patten's proposals violated the Basic Law and the previous agreements between China and Britain and that it should not be bound by his attempt to establish a *fait accompli*. Beijing has further argued that the system of elections chosen by Patten favours allegedly 'pro-British' candidates, or at least those who are likely to cause trouble to the HKSAR Executive.[27] Accordingly, Beijing is duty bound to replace them. Attention will focus mainly upon the latter as the principal legislative organ of government. Beijing has proposed to replace it with a provisional Legislative Council that will be empowered to enact laws, but whose principal purpose will be to devise a new system of elections so that a new Council could be elected preferably within a year.

It is possible that the Chinese authorities and representatives of the Democratic Party should establish a dialogue and reach an understanding before the due date of 1 July 1997. It will be recalled that this party and its allies enjoyed the support of the largest number of voters in the only two direct elections held in Hong Kong. It is nevertheless more likely that their representatives would be excluded altogether from the new provisional body. It would hardly inspire confidence among the people of Hong Kong and especially among the middle-class professionals (who proportionally voted in large numbers) if, as one of their first measures upon the reassertion of sovereignty, the Chinese authorities were to insist upon riding roughshod over the expressed wishes of the majority of the voters.

The provisional legislature could be expected to draw up a new electoral system based on a mix of proportional representation, functional constituencies of the old style with narrowly drawn franchises and some government appointees. But, on the basis of the votes cast in the 1991 and 1995 elections, the Democrats and their allies would still emerge as the largest political grouping in the new legislature. Short of actually rigging the elections, the only way that the Chinese authorities could ensure that this did not happen would be to disqualify the Democrats for lacking in 'patriotism'. Few moves could be more calculated to discredit the undertaking to allow Hong Kong to practice a 'high degree of autonomy'. A cowed and compliant legislature would soon undermine the independence of the judiciary which would find that laws on which controversial decisions had been based would be amended by the legislature to be more to the liking of the Chinese authorities.

Under such circumstances it may be assumed that those hundreds and thousands of business and professional people who could leave would do so earlier rather than later. Hong Kong would rapidly decline into being little more than China's best port. China and its new leaders would then face the whole range of deleterious consequences discussed earlier. Presumably the Chinese authorities would recognise in good time the implications of going too far in redressing what they consider to be the iniquities of the Patten legacy. They may also come to recognise that, although the legislature may have important powers, they are limited. For example, its bills can only take effect if signed and promulgated by the Chief Executive who cannot be removed except through the unusual and difficult process of impeachment. Even then the final decision would rest with the Central Peoples Government.[28]

The Basic Law also allows for circumstances under which the Chief Executive could be compelled to resign, but these actually illustrate the enormous powers of this office. Upon his or her refusal to sign a bill, the Legislative Council would then have to pass it with a two-thirds majority within three months. If there were still an impasse, the Chief Executive could dissolve the Legislative Council and call for new elections. If the pattern were repeated in the new Council, he or she would have to resign. The same procedure would apply if the Council were to refuse to approve an appropriation or any other important bill. Before reaching the point of resignation the Chief Executive could chose to compromise. Moreover, by that stage the Chief Executive, who will have reported to the Central Government, could invoke the threat of intervention by Beijing. In sum, the Chinese authorities could call upon the extensive powers of the Chief

Executive to obviate unwelcome acts undertaken by the Legislative Council. Failing that, they could disallow laws they consider to infringe the responsibilities of the Central Government or to encroach upon the relationship between that government and the Region.[29] In sum, there are good reasons as a matter of their own interests for the Chinese authorities to stop short of undermining the post-1997 Legislative Council.

The Chief Executive and relations with China

Much will depend on how the future Chief Executive will develop relations with the various Chinese authorities on the mainland. The question of liaising with Beijing and appropriate provinces, notably Guangdong, will be important in not only protecting the Region from untoward policies but in promoting cooperation. As the Hong Kong economy becomes more deeply integrated with the local and national Chinese economy, the question of how the two different political systems interact with each other will acquire greater importance.

Technically, the Chief Executive will be accountable to the Central Government as well as to the Region. According to the Basic Law and as confirmed recently by a senior official of the HKMAO in Beijing, the future HKSAR will not be subordinate to any departments of the Chinese Central Government or its provinces, autonomous regions and municipalities.[30] The Region will exercise independent executive, administrative and judicial authority except for the conduct of external defence and foreign affairs. It will not pay taxes to the Central Government.

In practice, however, the HKSAR will be greatly dependent on the mainland and it will fall to the Chief Executive to arrange working relations with both the central and regional authorities. Ideally, he or she will have to uphold the style appropriate to a highly legalised system of government while dealing with authorities on the mainland in which politics, bargaining, personal relationships and bureaucratic interests are of greater significance. The Chief Executive could not, for example, follow the age-old practice of Chinese regional leaders of 'feigning to comply' with the directives of the central authorities while in practice quietly proceeding with their own agendas. Such practices would soon run counter to the norms and methods of the civil service of Hong Kong and would risk eroding the Hong Kong system itself.

In seeking to promote the interests of the HKSAR, the Chief Executive will have to develop a method of approach that will take advantage of the direct access to the Central Government and to the leaders of, say, Guangdong Province. He or she would have to develop the necessary negotiating and political skills to utilise Hong Kong's bargaining strengths in dealing with different ministries and institutional interests. For example, the Chief Executive will probably develop close working relations with the Standing Committee of the National People's Congress to whom the HKSAR is required to report all its legislation which, as we have seen earlier, may be invalidated. That is the body which is most concerned with promoting the rule of law in China and may be seen as a 'natural ally' for certain purposes. In so far as the Chief Executive develops good working relations with the leaders of Guangdong Province, it may be found that their joint local interests could be best advanced by Guangdong's pursuit of practices appropriate to the mainland's domestic political system as the HKSAR negotiates with interested parties in the Central Government in accordance with its own legalistic style. In time, the Chief Executive will have to learn how to advance Hong Kong's interests by operating at both central and provincial levels in China.

Assuming that the Chief Executive will not be a member of the Communist Party, it is likely that the communist party leaders in Beijing will wish to place a senior and trusted member of the Party close to the Chief Executive. That would be in addition to communist party members who may operate from the NCNA and the Ministry of Foreign Affairs. How the Chief Executive may relate to that person would be important in determining his or her reception by China's central and provincial leaders and, indeed, the general approach of those leaders to the HKSAR. Clearly, the future prospects of the HKSAR will depend greatly upon the personal qualities of the Chief Executive, but residents will also look closely for evidence of the presence and influence of the communist party.

The seepage of corruption

There is a pervasive fear in Hong Kong that even if its 'way of life' were to survive intact during the initial period after the transfer of sovereignty, it could be undermined before too long by the spread of corruption from the mainland. The scale of the corruption in China is such that China's leaders have time and again warned that it could bring about the end of communist rule. It permeates all levels of the government and the communist party, and few business activities are free of it. It has, for example, led to local branches of the Chinese security organisations near Hong Kong to becoming engaged in smuggling and piracy.

Hong Kong itself has not been free of corruption, but since the establishment of the Independent Commission Against Corruption (ICAC) in 1972 and the Securities and Futures Commission (SFC) in 1988, official corruption and financial transgressions have been greatly diminished.[31] The international business and financial communities have shown confidence in the business and financial practices of Hong Kong. A large number of businesses in Hong Kong are already affected by the 'contagion' from China. Many examples could be cited. Relatively innocuous ones include the ways in which many local businesses at the suggestion of mainland interlocutors hire the offspring of senior Chinese officials as trainees; or at their initiative hire them as 'advisers' or 'consultants' who then receive payments into foreign bank accounts. The local businesses then hope to benefit from business contracts in China.[32] More seriously, perhaps, the ICAC (which has never published its detailed findings regarding China-related firms) estimated in 1991 that the cash and gifts paid to mainland firms to facilitate business transactions in China added between three and five per cent to business operating costs.[33]

The principal concern centres on the threat to the honesty and efficiency of the civil service and the probity of the judiciary. The problems of conducting business with China are not limited to Hong Kong, and local businesses will continue to be subject to the supervision of the ICAC and SFC. But should the civil service and the judiciary be corrupted, vital elements of the Hong Kong system would be corroded. In particular, concern has arisen about the treatment of mainlanders and Chinese firms by the government and its watchdogs. As we have seen, the ICAC has been reluctant to report on Chinese firms in Hong Kong. The territory has been the recipient of 'hot money' from China and it has become customary for Chinese firms to establish themselves in Hong Kong by indirect means. In fact, by the end of the 1980s, one of the NCNA-owned newspapers in Hong Kong complained that the relevant Chinese ministry was no longer able to keep track of the number of different firms operating with Chinese capital in Hong Kong.[34] More worrying (from the perspective of the probity of the civil service) is the expectation that the post-1997 government will be swayed into granting lucrative construction contracts to Chinese firms for other than strictly commercial reasons.

Finally, it is feared that the courts may be inhibited from deciding against politically well-connected Chinese in civil and criminal cases and against their enterprises in the event of contract disputes.[35]

Independence, censorship and intimidation

Although guaranteed by both the Joint Declaration and by the Basic Law, the freedoms of speech, publication and education have already become subject to self-censorship and intimidation by the Chinese authorities. This does not augur well for the future, for one of the distinctive features of Hong Kong over many years has been the freedom of the press and the free flow of information despite the absence of democracy. The Hong Kong government has, in the past, exercised a degree of censorship partly because of paternal prudishness and partly to avoid inflaming political sensitivities in China. But that has been generally regarded as an irritant rather than a major threat to liberty and free expression. Chinese measures in this regard are viewed as altogether more ominous. Hong Kong journalists have been jailed for long periods for what would be regarded as paltry offenses elsewhere. In one case, a journalist, Xi Yang, was sentenced for twelve years for disclosing an alleged financial secret that the central bank planned to sell off part of its gold reserves and that interest rates would not be raised for a third time that year. He was kept in custody for more than seven months during which time his only contact with the world outside was a thirty-minute visit by his father. His trial was held in secret and the family notified four days later. His informant was jailed for fifteen years.[36] Another case involved Jimmy Lai, a self-made millionaire and owner of a successful clothing chain who published a mass-circulation weekly, *Next Magazine* in which he took the opportunity to denounce the Chinese Premier, Li Peng, in crude terms. His successful shop in Beijing was promptly closed down. It reopened after he cut back on his ownership of the clothing chain. Jimmy Lai has since launched a mass-circulation *Apple Daily* which is backed by his considerable fortune. The Chinese authorities regularly exclude its journalists from their news conferences.[37]

One effect of such intimidation is what is regarded as a growing practice of self-censorship. There are many examples including the highly visible decision by the media magnate Rupert Murdoch to drop the BBC's 24-hour news channel from being broadcast on Star TV so as to curry favour with Beijing for commercial purposes. Others, less visible, include a number of Chinese language newspapers and even the previous so-called 'flagship of the colony'– the *South China Morning Post*. In early 1995 it abruptly stopped publishing a highly popular cartoon that severely satirised the malpractices of Chinese officials. For its part, the NCNA regularly advises Chinese firms to withdraw advertising from newspapers deemed to have been offensive. Newspaper owners and editors are often fêted and discretely cultivated while offending journalists are denounced as 'anti-China' or 'pro-British'.[38] These efforts have made their mark and they do not portend well for post-1997. Meanwhile, in the build-up to 1997, many important international media establishments have consolidated their positions or opened new bureaus in Hong Kong. The affairs of Hong Kong will be increasingly highlighted in the international media and placed before the scrutiny of the outside world. The Chinese authorities will have to act with greater caution if they are seek to give the impression that they are truly honouring their commitments in the Joint Declaration and the Basic Law. Moreover, the September 1995 elections showed that the Hong Kong middle-class professionals in particular have not been intimidated by such tactics. The Chinese side will have to be careful lest tactical victories over the local media do not become strategic setbacks in the wider world.

The international dimensions

At least two important factors must be considered. These include the preservation of Hong Kong's international personality and the influence that foreign powers may be able to exert on Beijing's conduct in Hong Kong.

Both the Joint Declaration and the Basic Law recognise that HKSAR will continue to enjoy a high degree of autonomy in the management of its external affairs. Within the framework in which (as the sovereign power) the PRC will exercise responsibility for foreign affairs, the Basic Law devotes a separate chapter to the conduct of external affairs by the HKSAR itself. As with the British arrangements, Hong Kong representatives will be able to participate as members of the delegation of the sovereign power in diplomatic negotiations affecting the Region that are conducted by the sovereign government. More importantly, however, the Basic Law allows for the HKSAR, using the name 'Hong Kong, China' to maintain and develop relations and conclude agreements with foreign states and regions and international organisations in what are termed 'appropriate fields, including the economic, trade, financial and monetary, shipping, communications, tourism, cultural and sports fields' (Article 151). The HKSAR will also be authorised to issue passports, travel documents and to regulate its own immigration controls. The HKSAR will also continue to be empowered to institute official and semi-official trade representation offices abroad. Foreign consular and other official or semi-official missions may remain and be established even where the relevant states do not have formal diplomatic relations with the PRC. But in such cases the approval of Beijing would be required.

These provisions, which have generally been accepted by the international community add up to an international personality that is in possession of considerable capacities. But in the absence of its own sovereignty, the HKSAR will not be an international legal personality. It will be something less than that, and a degree of ambiguity about it will remain. The critical factor will be the extent to which the executive, the judiciary and the legislature are properly constituted and able to discharge their responsibilities in accordance with the stipulations of the Joint Declaration and the Basic Law.

> If the HKSAR government is to be run on so short a leash from Beijing that it could exercise any significant degree of legislative, executive, or judicial autonomy, no amount of window dressing in diplomatic terms could salvage Hong Kong's international role.[39]

The question of external representation will also be important. The HKSAR and Beijing will have to establish a working relationship that will allow sufficient autonomy for Hong Kong's separate conduct of the range of external relations to be recognisably separate. Beijing is unlikely to allow continuation of the current practice in which foreign missions deal directly with individual departments of the Hong Kong government without reference to London or the office of the Political Adviser. For reasons of geography, economics, politics and security, Hong Kong is very important to Beijing in ways that were never true for London. Once again the question will be the balance that Beijing will choose to draw between the impulse to exercise control and the benefits available from honouring the pledge to allow 'a high degree of autonomy'. Both options entail risks for Beijing.

Finally, the role of foreign powers will be complex and difficult. Most of the Asian Pacific countries have important economic ties with Hong Kong that go beyond its role as a gateway to China. It is an important trading partner and a supplier of important financial services. However, the countries that matter most are Japan and, especially, the USA. As the major powers in the region as a whole, China's leaders necessarily pay much heed to them. Japan and the USA are the largest foreign investors in Hong Kong (apart from China) and tens of thousands of their citizens live and work there. More than a thousand Japanese firms have offices in Hong Kong and the USA is not far behind with 900. Hong Kong is an important trade partner for both countries and an important destination for Japanese tourists. There is no question that the two great countries have interests which they wish to uphold and promote in Hong Kong. On the whole that is not disputed by Beijing, and it has not reacted adversely to discrete comments made by Japanese and US leaders and senior officials on meeting their Chinese equivalents about their expectations of the Chinese side to abide by its agreements on Hong Kong.

Japan and the USA will necessarily take a closer interest in how the Chinese manage the transfer of sovereignty and its aftermath than Beijing will find congenial. They will both be interested to examine the degree of autonomy that the HKSAR will be allowed to exercise in practice. The less evidence there is of autonomy, the more reluctant the two will be to allow Hong Kong to continue to enjoy the special benefits and privileges of membership of international trade and policy bodies. In fact, a senior US official has already publicly alerted Beijing to the counter measures it would take under such circumstances.[40] For the present, some of the broader issues are in abeyance until the transfer of sovereignty is achieved. They encompass the significance of the relations of each of the two powers with China, the future of China and of the development of the Asia-Pacific as a whole.

Japan has a special interest in the stability of the region as a whole and in the emergence of a less bellicose China able and willing to become constructively engaged in the region. Its current problems with the Chinese government over nuclear and military issues allied to some of the deeper causes of mutual misapprehensions would be deepened by a failure over Hong Kong. It would exacerbate Japanese underlying fears and increase anxieties about Beijing's approach to Taiwan. A manifest failure in Hong Kong would probably damage the economic relations with China which have been central to the Sino-Japanese relationship. Any pressure from Japan will necessarily be discrete rather than bombastic, but it is one that China's leaders would not readily discount.

It is the USA, however, that will play the key role. This has been implicitly recognised by Beijing which, despite its complaints about unwanted US interference, has sent Lu Ping, Director of the HKMAO, to the main cities in the USA on two separate occasions (the last in March 1995) to explain China's policies.[41] In 1990, Congress enacted the Immigration Act which established a separate immigrant visa quota for Hong Kong and offers a deferred visa to Hong Kong residents with the object of providing refuge for the future without provoking an immediate departure, and in the hope that it will increase local confidence in the future. By an Act of Congress of 1992, the Secretary of State is required to report to Congress every eighteen months on the situation in Hong Kong, including the development of its democratic institutions.[42] The two reports so far issued by the State Department have been condemned by the Chinese side as interference in its domestic sovereign affairs. But the USA will clearly continue to exert pressure on China to abide by its agreements. There is evident pressure within Congress to place Hong Kong within the general framework of the application of human rights demands upon Beijing.

Since Hong Kong has traditionally been largely a British concern and the negotiations about its future purely a bilateral matter between London and Beijing, Hong Kong has not appeared very large on the agenda of Sino-US relations. But that could change rapidly in view of its broader significance. China will be keen to prevent this from becoming yet another obstacle in relations with the USA. However, in view of the broad range and significance of America's relations with China that include the problems of Korea, arms control and the proliferation of weapons of mass destruction, Taiwan, sea lanes in the South China Sea and the larger question of security in the Asia-Pacific, as well as many trade and economic matters, human rights issues etc., the US administration may be reluctant to add the problem of Hong Kong. But since the future of democracy in Hong Kong touches on so many questions dear to Congress and in view of the implications for Taiwan of a manifest Chinese failure in 1997, the USA may have little option but to become engaged. The intensity of its engagement will depend on many contingent factors, but the possibility of US engagement should provide the Chinese authorities with an additional incentive to make a success of the recovery of sovereignty in 1997.

Chapter 6

Conclusion
A turning point for China?

There can be no question that China's leaders intend to do their very best to make the recovery of sovereignty and the implementation of the policy of 'one country two systems' a resounding success. The main doubts centre on their capacity to resolve the political problems that arise from the enormities of the differences between the two systems. However, whether or not they are successful, the recovery of sovereignty over Hong Kong will be an important turning point in the political evolution of the People's Republic. If this first step towards the peaceful reunification should turn out badly it would, as argued earlier, damage the confidence in the new leaders, deepen China's problems with the outside world and could presage a period of turning inwards with incalculable consequences for the Chinese economy that could lead to social and political instability. Were the takeover to be accomplished with minimal disruption to Hong Kong, the immediate repercussions would be beneficial to China and its rulers. But if Beijing were to succeed in accomplishing a relatively smooth transfer of sovereignty new problems would arise. Before too long, however, the coexistence of the two systems within China would encourage the pluralistic tendencies already evident in the mainland and accentuate the maritime drift of China's economic and political geography. In time, Hong Kong would become an attractive example to many people in the cities up and down China who would wish to emulate its way of life including its system of government and freedom under the law.

The first steps, however, may be crucial and these are affected by additional problems. As we have seen, China's leaders have been troubled by their fears of possible British attempts to retain influence in Hong Kong beyond 1997 and by challenges from pro-democracy forces in Hong Kong that they have chosen to regard as subversive.

Consequently, the Chinese side is preparing to assert a degree of political control that was not envisioned in the Joint Declaration or even in the Basic Law. However, they have made economic plans that clearly require Hong Kong to be a separate entity.

Preliminary reports of the first drafts of the Ninth Five Year Plan (1996–2000) and what has been called the economic blueprint for 1996 to 2010 envisioned mainland China and Hong Kong as constituting separate independent economic entities. Reportedly, the draft stated:

> In the international arena, the two [the mainland and Hong Kong] will have independent developments; they will cooperate with each other and compete with each other.

It anticipated a mutually beneficial relationship between the mainland and the HKSAR providing that the latter could maintain 'its economic independence and autonomy'. The report noted,

> Hong Kong is not only the bridge through which the hinterland reaches the world; it is also the mainland's best partner in economic development.

The HKSAR will be expected to continue to help the mainland in raising funds and attracting investments of different kinds, especially in helping PRC *government units and enterprises* raise capital in world markets. That, in turn, should attract more international capital and foreign financial institutions to the HKSAR, further consolidating its position as an international financial centre. The HKSAR would serve the motherland by providing channels for Chinese products to reach the world market. Hong Kong businesses should help mainland factories and service units secure orders from overseas firms. The HKSAR should also help with 'beneficial contributions' to economic exchanges with Taiwan.[1]

Interestingly, the final version of the Plan that was published by the official news agency was more circumspect. Hong Kong and Macau were to retain their capitalist systems and 'style of life'. Hong Kong would retain its status as a free port and as an international financial and trading and shipping centre. As a separate tariff zone of China it would 'enjoy better economic mutual benefit and seek common development with the country's interior parts. This will not only be conducive to further promoting the stability and prosperity of Hong Kong and Macao, but also to socialist modernization construction of the interior'.[2] This rather curt reference to the future role of Hong Kong does not exclude the possibility that a more expansive role might be played as suggested in the preliminary report, but nor can it be said to be an imaginative response to the challenges and opportunities that closer relations with this economic powerhouse might provide.

The Five Year Plan and the 'Blueprint' may be seen as the products of central ministries and the advisers to central leaders. Accordingly, they tend to express interests associated with government units and state-owned enterprises rather than those of the more market-oriented non-state-owned sectors and the smaller scale labour intensive foreign-related enterprises associated with the bulk of the investments from Hong Kong and Taiwanese business people. The emphasis upon the state sector that is associated with administrative controls and state administrative interests may be seen to be in contradiction with the strictly commercial guidelines that have shaped the economic development and financial operations of Hong Kong. It tends to illustrate still further the gap in outlook and perhaps understanding that exists between Beijing and Hong Kong. It suggests that, just as Beijing hopes to use its industrial policy to direct the more market-oriented economy of mainland China, it similarly hopes that the Hong Kong economy will respond to its signals rather than to those of the marketplace. Indeed, it hopes that Hong Kong will be able to lead international investors in that direction.

There may indeed be Hong Kong firms and international companies that find Beijing's proposals attractive. But if that were to become as extensive in scope as Beijing seems to wish, it would be necessary in the first instance to offer proper financial incentives through, for example, the taxation system. That would have to be followed fairly soon by improving the administrative arrangements for the signing and implementation of contracts. More generally, the economy and enterprises would have to become more transparent in their operations and to follow rules that conform more closely to those common in the international economy. Beijing would have to modify significantly the current system by which ever changing administrative rules and guidelines were kept secret from foreign partners (potential and actual). The July 1995 measures that established the policy governing foreign investment were important moves in that direction, but more is required if Beijing is to attract the hundreds of billions of dollars of foreign investment that it claims to need. Hong Kong would not be able to play the critical role that Beijing anticipates without significant changes along these lines.

As we have seen, the depth and the timing of such changes and reforms have been issues around which powerful forces have contended in China since the reforms were initiated in late 1978 and constantly promoted by Deng Xiaoping since then. Indeed, these struggles go back to the disputes of the first reformers with their adversaries in the nineteenth century. The significance of the Deng reforms is that, despite these battles and occasional setbacks, the general drift has been to develop the reforms further rather than to reverse them. If China's vast economic problems are not to lead to instability and chaos, it will be necessary to maintain high economic growth rates in the years to come. This would suggest that rather than subordinating Hong Kong to the dictates of the mainland's central planners, it is they and their state-owned enterprises who will have to adapt to the demands of the international marketplace. China is not the only country in East Asia that is in need of massive investments and if it is to attract international finance it must compete. Thus, even within the framework being worked by Beijing, it is likely that Hong Kong will be play a critical role in promoting the course of reform as well as that of economic development.

The Ninth Five Year Plan and the 'Blueprint' for economic development to the year 2010 also address the problem of getting Hong Kong to serve the country as a whole and not just Guangdong. Conscious of the plans drawn up by provincial and municipal authorities in Guangdong for economic integration with Hong Kong, Beijing has prepared detailed recommendations for areas of close cooperation with the HKSAR including infrastructure, investment, human resources, trade and economic policy. Apparently, a State Council team that reports to Premier Li Peng was completing in September an elaborate report on cooperation with Hong Kong. Drafted by more than ten ministries and commissions, the document is said to be separate from the Five Year Plan. Reportedly, 'it looks at concrete, micro-level areas where cooperation between the mainland and the SAR economies can best take place'.[3]

In some ways, the Beijing proposals reflect current trends as leading Hong Kong businessmen and companies have invested in many parts of China including Shanghai, Wuhan and Tianjin even though the bulk of their investments is still directed towards Guangdong.[4] A modern highway and a new rail track are currently being built between Beijing and Hong Kong that are due to be completed around the time of the transfer of sovereignty. New economic opportunities are bound to emerge as a result. Beijing's success in transforming the contribution of Hong Kong investors from a focus on Guangdong Province that concentrates upon relatively small-scale labour intensive enterprises, real estate, hotels etc., into a country-wide scope that puts more emphasis on infrastructure will ultimately depend upon how attractive it is able to make this in strictly commercial terms.

Beijing's need to adapt to the commercial market-oriented conditions of Hong Kong is mirrored in the political world too. The tendency of Beijing to describe the future political relations as those 'between a parent and a child' carries connotations of the kind of filial obedience required by the Confucian code. It is reminiscent of the earlier proposition advanced by Beijing that the prosperity of the Hong Kong economy was dependent upon the Chinese economy. This was only part of the truth that the prosperity of both economies depended on each other. But perhaps more importantly, as recognised in the Five Year Plan and related documents, the significance of the economy in Hong Kong derives from its separate and independent character. It is its openness, its capitalist free market system and its international importance as a financial centre that are appreciated by Beijing.

If the kind of paternalism that Beijing displays on the economic front were to be paralleled on the political front, there would be less concern in Hong Kong and elsewhere about the future. For the success of the Hong Kong economy turns ultimately on the rule of law. The practice of freedom under laws openly published and impartially adjudicated has been the necessary condition for the development of the Hong Kong economy. Of course, it was only with the enterprise and hard work of the Chinese people of the region that the sufficient condition was supplied for the economy to flourish. The same was true of Shanghai for the hundred years before the communist takeover. But once the rule of law crumbled at the hands of bureaucracy and arbitrary communist party rule, Shanghai began to decay and the former backwater of Hong Kong became transformed as the gateway to and from China. Hong Kong has succeeded as the international meeting place or confluence of the different business practices of the Chinese Overseas, Western and multinational companies, and operators of international finance because of the probity of its legal system that also undergirds its administrative system that is generally admired for its efficiency and political neutrality.

Commercial contracts (as all contracts) in Hong Kong are ultimately subject to the law and to the courts that adjudicate upon disputes that may arise. It is this legal structure that provides the framework within which business is conducted. That is why so many Western companies that deal with China prefer to base their operations in Hong Kong rather than on the mainland where transactions depend upon relationships (*guanxi*) and politics. Similarly, the administration of government in Hong Kong is subject to a legal and constitutional framework. As noted by a legal expert on Hong Kong:

> In a common law system, government policy is either in legal form, that is in a statute, or it is not. If it is not, it is not law and must always be subordinate to or complementary to the law. It is never superior to the law. On the other hand, when policy is expressed in legal form it is law and must be obeyed. The very essence of constitutional government is that no person, policy in non legal form, institution, or political party is above the law.[5]

This condition has not applied on the mainland. Traditionally, law was not a restraint on government but an instrument of state for control of the population. Since the establishment of the PRC, law has been subordinate to the dictates of the CCP in both theory and practice. Consequently, as a prisoner of policy it has been both unpredictable and arbitrary.[6] If Hong Kong is to play the economic role required by China's central planners they will have to learn to accept the inviolability of the law in Hong Kong. It would only be a question of time before the rule of law would be eroded if officials began to interfere with the liberty of the citizen without proper legal authority. Unlike the situation in China, it would not be sufficient to invoke a higher authority unless that included proper legal authority that had been validly delegated.

Foreign investors would rapidly lose confidence if the rule of law were to be undermined. There is a view in Beijing that since the capitalist world is motivated by profit, the prospects of China's vast markets gives China's leaders extraordinary powers of leverage. But the prospect of profit is also conditioned by assessment of risk. Were confidence in the rule of law to be eroded the risks to business would rise correspondingly and hence the rate of profitability would also rise. In other words, Beijing would find it much more expensive to attract foreign investment.

Since the rule of law depends not only on an independent and impartial judiciary, but on a responsible and independent legislature, paternalistic Beijing will also have to consider most carefully the formation of its proposed provisional Legislative Council. The more closely it should conform to that elected by the majority of Hong Kong people in September 1995, the more legitimacy it would enjoy even as it prepares a new electoral system. In other words, it matters a great deal whether or not Beijing can bridge the yawning gap that currently exists between the outlook of its leaders and that of the majority of the people in Hong Kong.

As discussed in previous chapters, the stakes are very high for the new collective leaders in Beijing, especially as the next national congress of the CCP is due to take place only three to four months after the recovery of Hong Kong's sovereignty on 1 July 1997. If the transition were perceived to have been handled successfully, their standing would be high and they could be expected to dominate the congress. Their policy preferences would prevail and their supporters would be placed in the key positions. The general policy on Taiwan would also seem to have been vindicated and, more generally, the new leaders could hope to strengthen the economy and foreign economic relations, consolidate relations with the Chinese communities overseas, and improve China's relations with the USA, Japan and the Western world as a whole. Conversely, were the new leaders to be perceived to have failed, their domestic standing would be damaged and all the above benefits would turn sour leading to a more beleaguered truculent China. A possible economic downturn might follow which would sharpen China's many problems and bring about social and political instability.

From a deeper historical perspective, it may be said that China is undergoing a profound and comparatively rapid series of interrelated transformations and adaptations. It is in the process of moving from a command to a market economy; from a predominantly rural to a more urban country; from a continentalist inward looking state to one that incorporates a growing maritime orientation; from a self-reliant economy to an interdependent one; from a unitary ideological outlook to one of cultural diversity; from a centralised administration that favoured (or perhaps feigned) uniformity to a decentralised one that is acknowledging diversity; and from totalitarianism towards pluralism. The actual course of these gigantic changes is far from smooth and there will probably be many cross currents, delays and even reverses. But the general direction of development would seem to be set in the long run not only because of the requirements of the economy, but also because the past from which China is transforming itself is bankrupt. A return to an ideologically inspired communist party in charge of a command economy that imposes an inward-looking totalitarianism is no longer a viable option.

The recovery of Hong Kong, which may be said to exemplify all the modernising traits to which China is moving, is occurring at a time when it could play an exceptional role in easing China's painful transition. As Beijing's plans for the end of the decade and beyond show, Hong Kong is expected to be a bridge to the outside world. Of course, Beijing intends this to apply to economic relations. But as argued above, that could only work if Beijing were to allow the rule of law and all that that implies to operate as well. By allowing Hong Kong to coexist as a truly separate system, Beijing would provide an opportunity for China not only to flourish as it entered the next century, but it would facilitate the negotiation of the great transformations by a process of adaptation. Accordingly, the reversion of the sovereignty of Hong Kong to China will be a challenge not only to the people and institutions of Hong Kong, but it will be a profound test to the adaptability of the leaders, the institutions and people of China itself.

Postscript

The purpose of this postscript written in February 1996, five months after the completion of the main text, is to highlight the significant developments that have taken place since then. More importantly, the postscript will also try to identify the main questions to be resolved since the Chinese side became more active in January in determining the final period of the transition.

The general improvement in Sino-British relations that began in 1995 has continued into 1996 and has been marked by ministerial visits to each other's capitals which both sides have claimed as successful. President Jiang Zemin and Premier Li Peng gave the British Foreign Minister, Malcolm Rifkind, the signal honour of receiving him despite their evident anger at the simultaneous broadcast on British television of a documentary showing Chinese orphanages in an appalling light. In effect, they signalled their determination not to be deflected from demonstrating the high priority they now assigned to Hong Kong. Rifkind and his Chinese counterpart, Qian Qichen, reached agreement on matters that had been held up for a considerable time such as the much needed new container terminal CT9, and about the terms on which the new Hong Kong passports would now be issued. The new pragmatic approach and the speeding up of delayed business were evident in the subsequent meeting of the Joint Liaison Group. The Chinese side dispensed with the denunciation of Britain's alleged violations of previous agreements arising from the Patten reforms and rapidly reached agreement on five technical, but important, matters, such as localising laws and endorsing further air service agreements.

Both the British and Chinese sides took steps to upgrade their trade relations. The Chinese tended to claim that, now that the British were more cooperative over Hong Kong, it had become possible to bring the growth of bilateral trade more in line with that of the other main European countries. The British tended to present the two matters as separate. In any event, the British Minister of Trade and Industry visited Beijing in 1995 and his Chinese counterpart Mme Wu Yi visited Britain in February 1996 and was able to preside over the signing of trade and business deals to the value of $2.7 billion. Chinese officials were quick to make the connection between better relations over Hong Kong and improved opportunities for British business. For good measure they added that the large British investments and the British companies active in Hong Kong could expect to do well there in the future. In accordance with their dealings with other western countries, the Chinese were seeking to use their improved economic bargaining position for political gain. Whether or not China's leaders still adhered to the expressed belief of Deng Xiaoping that the real British motive in Hong Kong was mercenary, their approach was similar to their attempts elsewhere, such as with regard to the USA, where they sought to use western companies with interests in China as a means to bring pressure to bear on their home governments, to antagonise the Chinese government. As we have seen, such pressure in the past has not decisively affected Britain's Hong Kong policy, and it is unlikely to do so in the final run-up to the handover of sovereignty. Such progress that has been made is because of the deeply shared interests of both sides in a smooth transfer of sovereignty and in the future stability and prosperity of Hong Kong.

The two sides, however, still differ on two issues that each regards as critical to Hong Kong's future. These are the Bill of Rights and the Legislative Council. The British are much troubled by the evident Chinese determination to prepare legislation to rescind this Bill and to return to the situation where the previous draconian laws could be invoked to limit free expression in the territory. Those laws were not invoked in practice and were remnants from a previous era when the Hong Kong government feared the potentially disruptive activities of Nationalist or Communist activists. The Bill of Rights was introduced in the aftermath of the bloody Tiananmen incident to allay anxieties in Hong Kong and to build confidence that the customary civil liberties that Hong Kongers had enjoyed so far could be better protected by being justifiable. The Chinese side has continued to see this as potentially subversive in its implications and as involving a possible dilution of their sovereign authority. The Chinese negotiators hold that the general provisions in the Joint Declaration of 1984 and in the Basic Law of 1990 are sufficient and that the Bill is not necessary. In particular, there is strong aversion to any suggestion of being externally accountable to the UN Commission on Human Rights, not even to the extent of reporting to it from time to time – as is currently the practice of the (British) Hong Kong government. The Chinese position has aroused considerable concern in Hong Kong not only because of the fear that the new sovereign power may abuse human rights in the territory, but also because there may not be legal redress against perhaps unintended abuses of power by the new administration. The ramifications are disturbing to many, especially in view of the great difficulty that the prominent politician, Martin Lee, the leader of the United Democrats, experienced in 1995 under current legal conditions in finding solicitors willing to act for him in a libel suit against a senior official of the Hong Kong Xinhua Branch. It is felt that if the legal profession were constrained under current conditions it would be even more reticent in the future HKSAR, especially once the Bill of Rights was to be rescinded.

Perhaps even more serious is the concern about the Legislative Council (LEGCO). The Chinese side is pledged to introduce a provisional LEGCO to take office immediately upon the resumption of sovereignty. This means that it would have to be set up before then in order to prepare properly the legislation that the Chinese deem necessary to annul measures introduced unilaterally by the British Hong Kong government, such as the Bill of Rights and the Patten package of electoral reforms, plus any futher laws that they may deem necessary for their view of the proper functioning of the HKSAR. In the British view, this is a potential disaster in the making. The existing LEGCO was properly elected in September 1995 and it plays an important and active role in the governance of Hong Kong. For example, it works with the Executive in the preparation and passing of legislation, including the budget. Senior members of the Civil Service are in continual interaction with LEGCO members. Once the Chief Executive designate is appointed, he will expect the cooperation of the government as a whole (which includes the existing LEGCO) in familiarising himself with the tasks ahead. It is a recipe for conflict and confusion if LEGCO and its anti-body, the provisional LEGCO, were to exist side by side working on different priciples to different agendas, but calling on the cooperation of the same senior officials and Chief Executive designate. It is impossible to envision circumstances more conducive to undermining confidence in the run-up to the handover of sovereignty than a conflict of loyalty and authority such as this. Indeed, one senior British official, calling upon the previous imagery of the 'through train', has privately likened it to a derailment or a train crash.

It is possible to draw up ingenious schemes that could avoid the worst aspects of the impending crash. For example, much trouble could be averted if the Chinese were to choose all the existing members of LEGCO to serve as members of the provisional one (subject, of course, to their having been deemed by the Preparatory Committee to be qualified to serve in the government of the HKSAR). But that would require more cooperation between all the parties than is currently evident. It would also require the British side to participate in the effective dismantling of the democratic element (limited though it is) that had been introduced under the aegis of Governor Patten with the support of the majority of the Hong Kong people. Neither he, nor his ministerial colleagues in London, nor the leaders of the Labour opposition, who may well form the government in London in the last months of the transition, are willing to contemplate cooperation in the undermining of the fragile democratic legislature in Hong Kong. Washington is also opposed and there is no support in the British media for what would be seen as the final betrayal of Hong Kong.

For their part, the Chinese leaders are not ready yet to prepare for so far ahead, even though this will have to be decided in a matter of months. Their immediate Hong Kong agenda is very crowded indeed. In accordance with their pre-arranged timetable, they have begun to take active measures to prepare the territory for the transition. As envisioned in the Basic Law, a Preparatory Committee (PC) was duly appointed to begin work in January 1996 with the immediate task of choosing a committee of 400 Hong Kong residents to select a Chief Executive designate for approval by Beijing. The PC will also have to establish a mechanism for cooperating with the Liaison Office of the Hong Kong government, as agreed by Malcolm Rifkind and Qian Qichen in November 1995. Meanwhile, the PC will be subdivided into various functional sub-committees to facilitate the general repsonsi-bility of overseeing the territory's reversion to Chinese sovereignty. Yet at some stage later this year, presumably after the selection of the Chief Executive designate, the PC will have to turn its attention to the selection of members for the provisional LEGCO. If the British side cannot see its way to cooperating in the ending of the auhtority of the existing elected LEGCO, the Chinese side, as the future sovereign, cannot be expected to back away from the provisional LEGCO without weakening its own authority and legitimacy. It cannot be expected simply to accept at this stage a body introduced unilaterally by the British in the teeth of objections by the Chinese side who regarded the entire exercise as a violation of previous agreements.

In fact, the Chinese leaders could claim already to have acted with a degree of reasonableness that few of their critics anticipated. The 150 members of the PC include 94 Hong Kong residents. An editorial in the local *South China Morning Post* (not normally regarded as 'pro-Beijing') noted that, despite the exclusion of members of the Democratic Party, the local appointees 'should prove sufficiently broadly-based to embrace most shades of opinion in Hong Kong'. It added significantly: 'Compared with the yes-men and women who dominated the Preliminary Working Committee . . . they represent a substantial improvement.'[1] Nevertheless, the composition reflected Beijing's view of the relative significance of the various groups in Hong Kong. More than half of the 94 are wealthy local business people and the four 'pro-Beijing' political groups ended up with a total of 21 members as against six for the Liberal Party and the Association for Democracy and People's Livelihood. Moreover, should there be any doubt of Beijing's capacity to get its way on the PC, it should be noted that in addition to the 56 mainland members, 85 of the Hong Kong membership are current NPC deputies, members of the National Committee of the Chinese People's Political Consultative Conference, Hong Kong affairs advisers or Hong Kong district affairs advisers.[2]

The three key leaders, Jiang Zemin, Li Peng and Qiao Shi, took the opportunity of the formal establishment of the PC on 26 January 1996 to reiterate some of the long-standing Chinese positions that had not been aired recently so as to provide reassurance to the people of Hong Kong. Thus, they repeated the pledge not to send a single official from the mainland to the KHSAR to ensure that Hong Kong people alone would govern Hong Kong (*Gangren Zhigang*) and they said that, in addition to being patriotic, Hong Kong people should love Hong Kong. They also promised that the Chief Executive designate and his team would not exercise any power before the transfer of sovereignty and they reiterated that not a penny would be taken of Hong Kong's money. Their commitment to retaining the confidence of the 180,000 strong Civil Service was reinforced by Li Peng's assertion to Malcolm Rifkind that the choice of the Chief Executive would be influenced by the need to maintain continuity in the Civil Service. Meanwhile, a regular programme of informal meetings was arranged between senior civil servants in Hong Kong and Chinese officials. Since the

Chinese were committed to placing a contingent of the People's Liberation Army in the HKSAR, the authorities went out of their way to provide reassurance of a kind about the élite troop they had in mind: the commanders were of the top rank and included one who had studied at a military establishment in England; the garrison would be smaller than the one currently deployed by the British; and the soldiers were being coached in Cantonese and English as well as trained in the ways of the West and Hong Kong.

However, no amount of reassurance could disguise the fact that the Chinese side had deliberately overlooked members of the Democratic Party in the selection of members to the committees charged with responsibilities in the transitionary period. The deliberate rejection of the members of the party who had won the overwhelming majority of votes and the seats in the two openly contested LEGCO elections of 1991 and 1995 inevitably damaged the claims of these institutions to be truly representative. More seriously, it suggested that the chasm between the two sides could not be breached. It implied that Beijing rejected the viewpoint of the majority of the politically active people of Hong Kong as totally unacceptable. Curiously, the Chinese stance against the Democractic Party (DP) in Hong Kong was more severe than that adopted towards the Democratic Progressive Party (DPP) in Taiwan, whose members have been oopenly received in Beijing. While it is true that some of the members of the Democratic Party had been active members of an organisation that supported the student demonstrators and other advocates of greater democracy back in 1989, their main concern is with Hong Kong and there can be little doubt that the overwhelming majority, if not all, would accept the strictures implicit in the concept of 'one country two systems' – namely, that socialist China and capitalist Hong Kong should not interfere in each other's affairs. The DPP by contrast openly sought legal independence for Taiwan, which was not only unpatriotic, but downright traitorous in the eyes of Beijing as it involved nothing less than secession and the possible dismemberment of China.

It is difficult to believe that the Chinese authorities will continue obdurately to reject members of the DP. They may claim that the hundreds of thousands of professionals who voted for the DP will stay in Hong Kong, regardless of the degree to which their preferred way of life may be damaged and de-legitimised, as long as the opportunity to make money is unaffected. But if China's leaders were to rely on being able to respond appropriately in the event of the beginning of an exodus they could well find that they might be too late. Once an exodus were to begin it could rapidly turn into a flood as people would wish to dispose of their property earlier before prices collapsed in the absence of buyers. It is possible that China's leaders are still bound by Deng Xiaoping's strictures against the leaders of the DP whom he named as subversive back in 1989 and they may well be advised by the Xinhua Hong Kong Branch about the unacceptability of the DP. Nevertheless, as leaders who have already shown a capacity to adapt to what might be regarded as their pressing interests in the territory, it is entirely possible that before too long they will open lines of communication to the DP. They could do so in the first instance by appealing to those in the DP who were not involved in supporting the Tiananmen demonstrators. Indeed, they may hope in that way to split the DP. But they may also recognise the advantages of seeking to include all members of the DP. The HKSAR would command greater legitimacy at home and abroad if it were to include even those with whom Beijing disagreed. In any event the HKSAR, as under the current constitutional arrangements, is designed to be an executive-led government in which the legislature at the end of the day would exercise only limited powers. Moreover, the future HKSAR government would have enormous reserve powers to deal with any activity deemed to be subversive.

Without a reconciliation of some kind between the DP and the Chinese authorities, no real progress could be reached about the handling of the problems associated with the establishment of the provisional LEGCO. Since the existing LEGCO with its DP members plays an important and integral part in the governance of Hong Kong, it is difficult to see how the future Chief Executive designate would be able to prepare himself properly for the exercise of government unless a reconciliation of a kind could be reached between the two. Thus, the key to avoiding a dangerous, not to say catastrophic, constitutional crisis towards the end of the transitionary period may well be whether an accommodation can be reached between the DP and the Chinese authorities.

Meanwhile, Beijing would do well to pay attention to the under-currents evident in Hong Kong. There is understandable nervousness about the future. If pressed, people will voice concern about the spread of corruption and the immense difficulties the Chief Executive of the HKSAR will have in resisting 'requests' by senior mainland figures to waive regulations in favour of their dependants. Many will also voice doubts about the capacities of the legal system to resist similar pressures. In other words, they fear the erosion of the probity of the law and the government. Even more disconcerting, however, is the incipient fear and distrust that has crept into social and professional interactions. Mindful of the uncertainties about possible vindictiveness by the 'new masters', people have been more guarded about revealing their views to each other. In that respect the transfer of sovereignty is well on its way. Beijing could well find that, instead of ostracising the DP and its members, its best interests could well lie in cultivating them. The future of the HKSAR does not just depend on the local entrepreneurs (important though their role is); it also depends on the professionals and the ordinary people of Hong Kong who recognise the need to uphold their existing freedoms as central to their way of life and to the flourishing of their extraordinary city.

There can be not question, however, that China's leaders seek a successful transition of sovereignty in Hong Kong. In the winter of 1995–1996 when the domestic political pendulum has swung towards the 'Browns' in terms of a relatively conservative economic policy and the display of unyielding nationalist rhetoric and military displays against Taiwan, they have chosen a relatively moderate and accommodating approach towards Britain and Hong Kong. Despite dark predictions from many sources, the economy of Hong Kong and economic relations with the Chinese mainland have continued to prosper. There are real grounds to be optimistic about the future of the HKSAR. The approaching deadline of 1 July 1997 should impose its own pressure in bringing about a reconciliation between the Chinese authorities and the DP that could pave the way to resolving the problem of LEGCO. Perhaps too when the time comes to implement the concept of 'one country two systems', China's leaders will take heed of the advice of the former head of the Xinhua Hong Kong Branch, Xu Jiatun, who on 20 March 1988 was quoted in *Wen Wei Po* (one of the Communist newspapers in Hong Kong) as having spoken to a journal in Beijing about his Communist colleagues: 'They always judge capitalism by old standards. They do not notice its changes. Had I not worked in Hong Kong for four years, I would probably have entertained the same ideas as those comrades. In short, some of our colleagues know too little about and are too fearful of modern capitalism.'[3] China's leaders are engaged in a bold experiment without parallel in modern history and the degree of their success will be tested not only in terms of the well-being of Hong Kong, but in terms of the capacity of China to adapt still further to the norms and practices of international society.

Notes

INTRODUCTION: THE CHALLENGE AND THE OPPORTUNITY

1   BBC *Summary of World Broadcasts* (Henceforth, SWB) FE/2253/F1–4.
2   As related to the author in 1992 by a senior official of the Hong Kong Branch of the New China News Agency who had been a part of the Chinese team that prepared China's initial negotiating position in late 1981.
3   Sir Percy Cradock, who was then still Foreign Policy Adviser to Prime Minister John Major, having served his predecessor Margaret Thatcher in that role since 1984, told the author in the summer of 1992 that it had long been the intention of Mrs Thatcher to appoint a senior politician to be the last governor. Sir Percy, who had advised both Prime Ministers against such an appointment in principle, thought that they might have been swayed by the example of the role played by Lord Soames in the lead-up to the independence of Zimbabwe.

1 THE SIGNIFICANCE OF HONG KONG

1   The contemporary figures are drawn from the 'Address by the Governor, the Rt. Hon. Christopher Patten, at the opening of the 1994/95 Session of the Legislative Council, 5 October 1994' (Hong Kong Government Printer) p. 25.
2   The best of these are Jan Morris, *Hong Kong* (NY: Vintage Books, 1989) – first published in 1985; Dick Wilson, *Hong Kong! Hong Kong!* (London: Unwin Hyman, 1990); and Kevin Rafferty, *City on the Rocks* (London: Penguin, revised edn. 1991).
3   Interview by the author with Sir Percy Cradock in June 1992. See also his account in *Experiences of China* (London: John Murray, 1994) pp. 180, 190.
4   Wilson (op. cit.) p. 34 for the value of remittances and Carl Riskin, *China's Political Economy* (Oxford: Oxford University Press, 1987) p. 208 for the statistics on China's foreign trade, 1965–1975.
5   For a detailed analysis, see Robert Ash and Y.Y. Kueh, 'Economic integration within Greater China: trade and investment flows between

China, Hong Kong and Taiwan' *The China Quarterly* (Special issue: *Greater China*, December 1993, no. 136) pp. 711–45.

6   The Editorial Board of The Almanac of China's Foreign Economic Relations and Trade, Beijing, *Almanac of China's Foreign Economic Relations and Trade 1994* (Hong Kong: China Resources Advertising Co. Ltd. 1995) p. 475.

7   *Ibid.*, pp. 313–466.

8   5 October 1994 Address to the Hong Kong Legislative Council (op. cit.) pp. 25–6.

9   Cited in Kevin Rafferty (op. cit.) p. 492.

10 Cited by Gerald Segal, 'Tying China into the international system' *Survival* (vol. 37, no. 2, Summer 1995) p. 61.

11 See the accounts of the evolution of thinking in Taiwan in Ralph N. Clough, *Reaching Across the Taiwan Strait, People to People Diplomacy* (Boulder: Westview Press, 1993) chapter 7, pp. 125–50; and Harry Harding, 'Taiwan and Greater China' in Robert G. Sutter and William R. Johnson (eds) *Taiwan in World Affairs* (Boulder: Westview Press, 1994) pp. 256–7.

12 *Almanac of China's Foreign Economic Relations and Trade 1994/95* (op. cit.) pp. 467–9.

13 For extended treatment of the phenomenon, see *The China Quarterly* (Special issue: *Greater China*, December 1993, no. 136).

14 Dick Wilson, *China, The Big Tiger* (London & NY: Little Brown, 1996) pp. 397–8.

15 Harry Harding, 'The concept of "Greater China": themes, variations and reservations' (*ibid.*) pp. 666–7.

16 Michael Yahuda, 'The foreign relations of Greater China' (*ibid.*) pp. 688–9.

17 Wilson, Hong Kong! Hong Kong! (op. cit.) chapter 4, pp. 31–41.

18 Cited by Yahuda (op. cit.) p. 690.

19 Rafferty (op. cit.) chapter 2, pp. 12–51.

20 Frank Welsh, *A History of Hong Kong* (London: HarperCollins, 1994) pp. 452, 461.

21 Wang Gungwu, 'Greater China and the Chinese Overseas' *The China Quarterly* (Special issue: *Greater China* December 1993, no. 136) p. 928.

22 *Ibid.*, pp. 934 and 938, respectively.

23 For analyses of these cycles, see R. Baum, *Burying Mao: Chinese Politics in the Age of Deng Xiaoping* (Princeton, NJ: Princeton University Press, 1994) pp. 5–9; and Kenneth Lieberthal, *Governing China: From Revolution Through Reform* (NY & London: W.W. Norton & Co., 1995) pp. 137–44 and the 'Boom bust cycle' pp. 269–73.

24 'A survey of China' *The Economist* (18 March 1995), survey p. 9.

25 Baum (op. cit.) pp. 231–2, and Merle Goldman, *Sowing the Seeds of Democracy in China: Political Reform in the Deng Era* (Cambridge, MA: Harvard University Press, 1994) pp. 257–60.

26 These colour labels were suggested to me by Harry Harding.

27 For the classic account of the attempt at reform by the nineteenth-century Confucians, see Mary C. Wright, *The Last Stand of Chinese*

Conservatism: The T'ung Chih Restoration, 1862–1874 (Stanford: Stanford University Press, 1957).

28 See David S.G. Goodman, 'Reforming China: foreign contacts, foreign values?' *The Pacific Review* (vol. 5, no. 1, 1992).

29 For a treatment that sees greater continuities in modern Chinese history and that does not stress the fault lines identified here, see the justly praised, Jonathan Spence, *The Search for Modern China* (London: Hutchinson, 1990).

30 Carsten Herrmann-Pillath, 'Economic development and institutional change: vacillating at the crossroads' in Lo Chi Kin, Suzanne Pepper and Tsui Kai Yuen (eds) *China Review 1995* (Hong Kong: Chinese University Press, 1995), especially pp. 19.30–19.38.

31 *Ibid.*, p.19.37.

32 The statistics for China are taken from 'Report on the implementation of the 1994 plan for national economic and social development and the draft 1995 plan for national economic and social development' *Beijing Review* (nos. 14–15, 3–16 April, 1995), centrefold p. iii. The Hong Kong figure is from *Hong Kong 1995* (Hong Kong: Government Printer, 1995) p. 489.

33 Bernard H.K. Luk, 'Hong Kong's international presence' in Donald McMillen and Man Si-wai (eds) *The Other Hong Kong Report 1994* (Hong Kong: Chinese University Press, 1994) p. 435.

34 James T.H. Tang, 'Hong Kong's international status' *The Pacific Review* (vol. 6, no. 3, 1993) p. 208.

35 *Ibid.*, pp. 211–13.

2 DIFFERENCES BETWEEN THE HONG KONG AND CHINESE SYSTEMS

1 Kevin Rafferty, *City on the Rocks: Hong Kong's Uncertain Future* (London: Penguin, revised edn. 1991) p. 492.

2 From author's interviews with various journalists and officials attached to the Xinhua News Agency and its related newspapers in Hong Kong.

3 For a brief note of their importance, see Kenneth Lieberthal, *Governing China: From Revolution Through Reform* (NY: W.W. Norton & Co., 1995) pp. 196–7. For more extended treatments, see A. Doak Barnett, *Cadres, Bureaucracy and Political Power in Communist China* (NY: Columbia University Press, 1967) and Lynn T. White III, *Policies of Chaos: The Organizational Causes of Violence in China's Cultural Revolution* (Princeton, NJ: Princeton University Press, 1989).

4 Sergei Goncharov, John W. Lewis and Xue Litai, *Uncertain Partners: Stalin, Mao and the Korean War* (Stanford: Stanford University Press, 1993) p. 40.

5 *Ibid.*, p. 100

6 For a close examination of these issues based primarily on American archives, see Nancy Bernkopf Tucker, *Patterns in the Dust: Chinese American Relations and the Recognition Controversy, 1949–1950* (NY: Columbia University Press, 1983).

7   Frank Welsh, *A History of Hong Kong* (London: HarperCollins, 1993) p. 443.

8   Cradock (op. cit.) p. 162.

9   For an account of Sino-British relations at this time, see James T.H. Tang, *Britain's Encounter with Revilutionary China, 1949–1954* London: Macmillan, 1992).

10 Nancy Bernkopf Tucker, *Taiwan, Hong Kong and the United States, 1945–1992: Uncertain Friendships* (NY: Twayne Publishers, 1994) pp. 200–8; and Welsh (op. cit.) pp. 444–50.

11 Welsh (op. cit.) p. 452–3.

12 Tucker, *Taiwan, Hong Kong and the United States* (op. cit.) p. 209.

13 *Ibid.*, p. 211.

14 Dick Wilson cites officials conceding the point after a sudden influx of refugees in 1962 *Hong Kong! Hong Kong!* (op. cit.) pp. 196–7.

15 Cited in Welsh, (op. cit.) p. 465.

16 Cradock (op. cit.) p. 162.

17 *Ibid.*, pp. 471–2.

18 *Ibid.*, pp. 433–40. See also S. Tsang, *Democracy Shelved* (Hong Kong: Oxford University Press, 1988).

19 N.J. Miners, *The Government and Politics of Hong Kong* (Hong Kong: Oxford University Press, fifth edition, 1994) pp. 21–2.

20 *Ibid.*, p. 32.

21 *1971 Hong Kong Annual Review*, p. 2 cited by Welsh (op. cit.) p. 461.

22 Lau Siu-Kai and Kuan Hsin-Chi, 'The changing political culture of the Hong Kong Chinese' in Joseph Cheng (ed.) *Hong Kong in Transition* (Hong Kong: Oxford University Press, 1986) p. 26.

23 Miners (op. cit.) p. 94

24 Cited *ibid.*, p. 36.

25 Dick Wilson, *Hong Kong! Hong Kong!* (op. cit.) p. 73.

26 For a careful and balanced survey, see Miners, (op. cit.) chapters 13 and 15. For a critical account by a former senior civil servant, see John Walden, *Excellency, Your Gap is Growing: Six Talks on a Chinese Takeaway* (Hong Kong: All Noble Co. Ltd., 1987).

27 See the discussion Lau Siu-kai and Kuan Hsin-chi, *The Ethos of the Hong Kong Chinese* (Hong Kong: Chinese University Press, 1988) pp. 178–87; and Lau Siu-kai, Kuan Hsin-chi and Wan Po-san, 'Political attitudes' in Lau Siu-kai, Lee Ming-Kwan, Wan Po-san and Wong Siu-lun (eds) *Indicators of Social Development: Hong Kong 1988* (Hong Kong: Hong Kong Institute of Asia-Pacific Studies, Chinese University of Hong Kong, 1991) pp. 173–205, especially pp. 177–8.

28 David Tang, cited by the knowledgeable Dick Wilson as the only Hong Konger he had come across who had done so in his *Hong Kong! Hong Kong!* (op. cit.) p. 48.

29 Li Ruihuan's address to the Hong Kong and Macao representatives at the CPPCC on 13 March 1995 was carried in full in the Hong Kong communist-controlled newspaper *Wen Wei Po*, available in English translation in BBC *SWB FE/2253/F1–4*.

30 Thomas B. Gold, 'Go with your feelings: popular culture in Greater China' *The China Quarterly* (December 1993, no. 136) pp. 907–25. See

also Orville Schell, *Mandate of Heaven: A New Generation of Entrepre-neurs, Dissidents, Bohemians, and Technocrats Lays Claim to China's Future* (NY: Simon & Schuster, 1994).

31 For a thoughtful account of this commercialised culture, see Chan Hoi-man, 'Culture and identity' in Donald H. McMillen and Man Si-wai (eds) *The Other Hong Kong Report 1994* (Hong Kong: Chinese University Press, 1994) chapter 12, pp. 443–68.

32 For accounts of these groups and the emergence of political parties, see Miners, (op. cit.) chapters 13 and 14.

33 According to official statistics, only about fifteen per cent of the labour force belong to some 450 trade unions. These are split in their political affiliations.

34 Lau Siu-kai and Kuan Hsin-chi, *The Ethos of the Hong Kong Chinese* (op. cit.) cited by Dick Wilson (op. cit.) p. 45.

35 Much of this paragraph is drawn from Paul C.K. Kwong, 'Internatio-nalization of population and globalization of families' in Choi Po-king and Ho Lok-sang (eds) *The Other Hong Kong Report 1993* (Hong Kong: Chinese University Press, 1993) chapter 10, pp. 147–74.

36 H.D.R. Baker, 'Life in the cities: the emergence of Hong Kong Man' *The China Quarterly* (September 1983, no. 95) pp. 469–79; and 'Social change in Hong Kong: Hong Kong Man in search of majority' *The China Quarterly* (December 1993, no. 136) pp. 864–77.

37 For some of the international political implications of these develop-ments, see Gerald Segal, *The Fate of Hong Kong* (London: Simon & Schuster, 1983) chapters 7–9, pp. 112–50.

38 *Hong Kong 1995* (Hong Kong: Government Printing Department, 1995).

39 For accounts of the conservative or 'leftist' perspectives as argued in the mid-1980s and early 1990s respectively, see Richard Baum, *Burying Mao: Chinese Politics in the Age of Deng Xiaoping* (Princeton, NJ: Princeton University Press, 1994) pp. 178–88 and 341–68.

3 THE TROUBLED NEGOTIATIONS

1 This chapter draws substantially on my article 'Hong Kong's future: Sino-British negotiations, perceptions, organization and political cul-ture' *International Affairs* (vol. 69, no. 2, April 1993).

2 The actual historical experiences of China with foreign political com-munities have been more varied and complex than current myths would allow. For brief but illuminating analyses, see Michael Hunt, 'Chinese foreign relations in historical perspective' in Harry Harding (ed.) *China's Foreign Relations in the 1980s* (New Haven, CN: Yale University Press, 1984) chapter 6; and William C. Kirby, 'Traditions of centrality, authority, and management in modern China's foreign relations' in Thomas W. Robinson and David Shambaugh (eds) *Chinese Foreign Policy: Theory and Practice* (Oxford: Clarendon Press, 1994) chapter 2.

3 Many important dimensions of this are captured in a series of essays that trace the ways in which the European experience of international relations has spread worldwide. See Hedley Bull and Adam Watson

(eds) *The Expansion of International Relations* (Oxford: Clarendon Press, 1984).

4   Welsh (op. cit.) p. 472.

5   This account draws on Robert Cottrell, *The End of Hong Kong: The Secret Diplomacy of Imperial Retreat* (London: John Murray, 1993) chapter 3, pp. 35–57; Percy Cradock, *Experiences of China* (London: John Murray, 1994) chapter 16, pp. 160–73; and Mark Roberti, *The Fall of Hong Kong: China's Triumph and Britain's Betrayal* (NY: John Wiley & Sons, 1994) chapter 2, pp. 15–24. These three books together with accounts in the weekly Hong Kong journal, *The Far Eastern Economic Review*, have been used in preparing the historical review as a whole.

6   Cited by Jurgen Domes, 'The impact of Hong Kong on PRC domestic politics' in Jurgen Domes and Yu-ming Shaw (eds) *Hong Kong: A Chinese and International Concern* (Boulder: Westview Press, 1988) p. 88.

7   Roberti (op. cit.) pp. 202–10 maintains that a deal to this effect was struck between Beijing and the then Governor Sir David Wilson.

8   Cradock (op. cit.) p. 244.

9   Percy Cradock, *Experiences of China* (London: John Murray, 1994) p. 266.

10 See, for example, David Shambaugh, *Beautiful Imperialist: China Perceives America, 1972–1990* (Princeton, NJ: Princeton University Press, 1991); and Allen S. Whiting, *China Eyes Japan* (Berkeley, CA: University of California Press, 1989).

11 Deng Xiaoping on 23 November 1989, see *Selected Works of Deng Xiaoping, Vol. III (1982–1992)* (Beijing: Foreign Languages Press, 1994) p. 33.

12 *The Selected Works of Mao Tsetung* Vol. V (Beijing: Foreign Languages Press, 1977) p. 361.

13 Cradock (op. cit.) pp. 210–11.

14 See the accounts of Cottrell (op. cit.) pp. 56, 60–2; and Roberti (op. cit.) p. 23.

15 Cradock (op. cit.) p. 188.

16 Cottrell (op. cit.) p. 61 notes the British failure to interpret Deng's original signals clearly. He further notes (p. 71) that the senior British advisers sought to persuade Mrs Thatcher on 28 July (after her victory in the Falklands) of the necessity of reaching a compromise with China on the basis of giving up sovereignty in return for continued British administration. Yet not only had Deng hinted earlier that with Taiwan in mind he sought an altogether different solution, but he had specifically told Edward Heath this in the hearing of Ambassador Cradock who was one of the officials advising Mrs Thatcher on that day in July. For his account, see Cradock (op. cit.) pp. 171–3.

17 Deng's claim has been independently confirmed to me by more than one British official who was present on the occasion.

18 Respectively, author's interview with Sir Percy Cradock in London, June 1992, and with a senior official in the Xinhua News Agency in Hong Kong, August 1992.

19 *Ta Kung Pao*, 16 October 1992, in BBC *SWB* FE/1515 A2/3.

20   This general point was made privately to me by a senior British official in May 1995.
21   This has been a perpetual theme in my various discussions with scholars and researchers of all ages in public and in private during the course of many visits to Beijing since 1990 when I first began to enquire into the character of the Sino-British negotiations.
22   Ambrose Y.C. King, 'Hong Kong talks...' in Domes and Shaw (eds) *Hong Kong* (op. cit.) p. 51.
23   Author's notes from discussions with researchers at the Chinese Academy of Social Sciences, August 1992.
24   See the remarks to this effect by the most senior and venerable leaders Deng Xiaoping, Chen Yun and Peng Zhen, cited in the Hong Kong newspaper *Hsin Pao*, 27 November 1992, in BBC *SWB* FE/1552 A2/4–5.
25   They found support from an unexpected source in the person of Lee Kuan Yew, the Senior Minister from Singapore (see the *South China Morning Post*, 15 December 1992).
26   Discussions that the author had with various scholars and officials in Beijing in September 1994 and June 1995.
27   Sir Percy Cradock has much to say about this in the course of his account of the negotiations (Part Three of his book op. cit.). The two standard studies of China's approach to negotiations are: Richard Solomon, 'Friendship and obligation in Chinese negotiating style' in Hans Binnendijk (ed.) *National Negotiating Styles* (Washington, DC: Foreign Service Institute, US Department of State, 1987) and Lucian W. Pye, *Chinese Commercial Negotiating Style* (Cambridge, MA: Oelgescher, Gunn & Hain, 1982).
28   Cradock (op. cit.) pp. 144, 198–204.
29   Cradock (op. cit.) p. 187.
30   This was done in a less than comprehensive way by an 'Assessment Office'. For details, see Roberti (op. cit.) pp. 121–3.
31   Ambrose Y.C. King, 'The Hong Kong talks and Hong Kong politics' in Domes and Shaw (eds) (op. cit.) p. 51.
32   Roberti (op. cit.) pp. 205–9.
33   For an analysis, see Joseph Fewsmith, 'Neoconservatism and the end of the Dengist era' *Asian Survey* (vol. XXXV, no. 7, July 1995) pp. 635–51.
34   Based on the author's interviews with Galsworthy and Ehrman in Hong Kong in July 1992 and with Lu Ping in Beijing in August 1992.
35   Author's interviews with scholars and officials in Beijing.

4   PROBLEMS OF THE LAST PHASE OF TRANSITION

1   Percy Cradock, *Experiences of China* (London: John Murray, 1994) p. 198; and Robert Cottrell, *The End of Hong Kong: The Diplomacy of Imperial Retreat* (London: John Murray, 1993) p. 148.
2   Cradock (op. cit.) pp.192–3.
3   The author's discussions in Beijing in February 1995 with scholars from the Chinese Academy of Social Sciences and the Institute of Contemporary International Relations.

4   For accounts of the NCNA and its activities, see Brian Hook, 'The external relations of Hong Kong' in Sung Yun-wing and Lee Ming-kwan (eds) *The Other Hong Kong Report 1991* (Hong Kong: Chinese University Press, 1991) pp. 505–9; and especially the article by John Burns, in John P. Burns, Victor C. Falkenheim and David M. Lampton (eds) *Hong Kong and China in Transition* (Toronto: Canada and Hong Kong Papers No. 3, Joint Centre for Asia and Pacific Studies, 1994).

5   For an account of the foreign policy bureaucracies in the early 1980s, see A. Doak Barnett, *The Making of Foreign Policy in China* (Boulder: Westview Press, 1985).

6   Cited by Christine Loh, 'The implementation of the Sino-British Joint Declaration' in Donald H. McMillen and Man Si-wai (eds) *The Other Hong Kong Report 1994* (op. cit.) p. 70.

7   For an account of Liao's significance, especially in relations with Japan, see Kurt Werner Radtke, *China's Relations With Japan, 1945–83: The Role of Liao Chengzhi* (Manchester: Manchester University Press, 1990). His significance as the drafter of the '12 Points' was pointed out to the author by an official of the NCNA, Hong Kong in July 1992.

8   See the accounts scattered throughout Cottrell (op. cit.) and especially Cradock (op. cit.) that make it abundantly clear that all the important questions were settled by Deng Xiaoping personally.

9   Carol Lee Hamrin, 'Elite politics and the development of China's foreign relations' in Thomas W. Robinson and David Shambaugh (eds) *China's Foreign Relations* (op. cit.) p. 89. See also her broader discussion pp. 70–112.

10   Beijing, Foreign Languages Press, 1993.

11   Interviews with author in London, July 1994, and Hong Kong, September 1994.

12   Qiao Shi was among the leaders who commented on the tenth anniversary of the Joint Declaration. See BBC *SWB* FE/2183/F1, 20 December 1994.

13   Li Ruihuan in BBC *SWB* FE/2253/FE1–4.

14   Reported by the respected Hong Kong newspaper *Ming Pao*, 21 June 1995, in BBC *SWB* FE/2339 G/4–5.

15   See 'Intelligence' in *Far Eastern Economic Review* (henceforth *FEER*) (23 February 1995) p. 12.

16   See speeches of late June carried in BBC *SWB* FE/2337/F1 and FE/2338/F1–2.

17   Louise do Rosario, 'Together at last, secret Beijing trip for top civil servant' *FEER* (20 July 1995) p. 28.

18   David M. Lampton, 'America's China policy in the age of the finance minister: Clinton ends linkage' *The China Quarterly* (No. 139, September 1994) pp. 597–621; and Harry Harding, 'Asia policy to the brink' *Foreign Policy* (No. 96, Fall 1994) pp. 57–74.

19   BBC *SWB* FE/2396/F1–2.

20   See, for example, the article by the Chairman of the highly placed China Institute for International Strategic Studies, Xu Xin, 'Who has threatened whom after all?' *International Strategic Studies* (no. 2, 1995) pp. 1–5.

21   See, for example, Shigeo Hiramatsu, 'China's naval advance: objectives and capabilities' *Japan Review of International Studies* (vol. 8, no. 2, Spring 1994) pp. 118–132.
22   Murray Hiebert, 'Comforting noises' *FEER* (10 August 1995) pp. 14–16.
23   Interview by the author with a leading scholar in the Institute of Asia-Pacific Studies, the Chinese Academy of Social Sciences, July 1995.
24   This account is based on interviews with British and Hong Kong government officials in August 1995.
25   Interview with author.
26   This point about the lack of subordinate status was made explicitly by a senior official of the HKMAO in an interview with the author in July 1995.
27   British officials in Hong Kong have privately told the author that Zhou Nan, the Director of NCNA, has been trying to resist proposed changes to his organisation.
28   Dick Wilson, *HongKong! Hong Kong!* (op. cit.) pp. 207–8.
29   For these two suggestions, see Mark Roberti, *The Fall of Hong Kong* (op. cit.) p. 308.
30   Interviews with author on 27 and 28 January 1995.
31   *International Herald Tribune* and *The Times* (London), 25 September 1995.
32   *Hong Kong: a Thousand Days and Beyond. Address by the Governor, the Rt. Hon. Christopher Patten at the opening of the 1994/95 Session of the Legislative Council* (Hong Kong: Government Press, 5 October 1994) pp. 27–34.
33   *Ibid.* p. 29.
34   Translated in BBC *SWB* FE/2337/F1–4.
35   Author's interviews in Beijing in July 1995.
36   For the 1985 figures, see Lau Siu-kai and Kuan Hsin-chi, *The Ethos of Hong Kong* (Hong Kong: Chinese University of Hong Kong, 1988) p. 84; and for the 1994 figures, see Michael E. DeGolyer, 'Politics, politicians and political parties' in Donald H. McMillen and Man Si-wai (eds) *The Other Hong Kong Report 1994* (Hong Kong: Chinese University Press, 1994) p. 83.
37   DeGolyer, *ibid.*, p. 89–90.
38   *Ibid.*, p. 81.
39   Christine Loh, 'The implementation of the Sino-British Joint Declaration' in *The Other Hong Kong Report 1994* (op. cit.) p. 70.
40   According to the Hong Kong newspaper, *Lien Ho Pao* (29 August 1995) in BBC *SWB* FE/2395G/10.
41   Louise do Rosario, 'Follow the leader: China grooming its own administration for Hong Kong' *FEER* (23 February 1995) p. 18.
42   *Ibid.*, p. 18.
43   Meeting Point chairman (which has merged with the United Democrats to form the Democrats of Hong Kong) Anthony Cheung, cited in Christine Loh 'The implementation of the Sino-British Joint Declaration' (loc. cit.) p. 70.
44   Interviews with author in July 1995.
45   For a clear account, see Miners, (op. cit.) chapters 8–10.

1   Deng Xiaoping, *On the Question of Hong Kong* (Beijing: Foreign Languages Press, 1993) p. 67, n. 1.
2   Li Hongzhang (1823–1901), the high official of the late Qing Dynasty, has been regarded by western scholars as a great statesman who sought to preserve China and its Confucian mores at a time when a weaker and decaying China was subject to attacks by more powerful and more modern states. China's nationalistic histories have subsequently regarded him as a betrayer of China's sovereignty and territorial integrity. The official note in Deng's *Selected Works* refrains from explicitly condemning him, but after describing his official position and responsibilities goes on to state:

> On behalf of the Qing government he presided over the signing of unequal treaties.... Under the terms [of which] China relinquished sovereignty, ceded territory and paid indemnities.

The note listed five such treaties but, curiously, it omitted the one involving the 1898 lease relevant to Hong Kong. Deng Xiaoping's insistence upon not going down in history as 'another Li Hongzhang' was so marked that British negotiators subsequently commented upon this to the author as they ruefully acknowledged that, at the beginning, they had not recognised how deeply the Chinese commitment to sovereignty was felt.
3   *Selected Works of Deng Xiaoping, Vol. III (1982–1992)* (Beijing: Foreign Languages Press, 1994) p. 23. It can also be found in Deng Xiaoping, *On the Question of Hong Kong* (Beijing: Foreign Languages Press, 1993) pp. 1–2. Both are translations from the Chinese edition published in October 1993.
4   Deng Xiaoping, *Fundamental Issues in Present-Day China* (Beijing: Foreign Languages Press, 1987). For no reason that the author has been able to ascertain, this volume also omitted Deng's 'Speech at a meeting with the Members of the Committee for Drafting the Basic Law of the Hong Kong Special Administrative Region' of 16 April 1987. This speech reaffirmed the basic points of Deng's approach to reform in China and his distrust of western-style democracy, even as applied to Hong Kong.
5   Allen S. Whiting, 'Chinese nationalism and foreign policy after Deng' *The China Quarterly* (no. 142, June 1995) pp. 295–316. See also the account in Baum, *Burying Mao* (op. cit.) pp. 330–56.
6   For a fascinating analysis of the frustrations underlying the nationalistic moods of contemporary Chinese society, see Geremie R. Barme, 'To screw foreigners is patriotic: China's avant-garde nationalists' *The China Journal* (no. 34, July 1995) pp. 209–34.
7   The complexities of regionalism in China are explored in David S.G. Goodman and Gerald Segal (eds) *China Deconstructs: Politics, Trade and Regionalism* (London: Routledge, 1994). See, in particular, David S.G. Goodman, 'The politics of regionalism: economic development, conflict and negotiation', and David S.G. Goodman and Feng Chongyi,

'Guangdong: greater Hong Kong and the new regionalist future' pp. 1–20 and pp. 177–201, respectively.

8   Geremie R. Barme, (op. cit.) p. 213.

9   David J. Clark, 'The Basic Law: one document two systems' in Ming K. Chan and David J. Clark (eds) *The Hong Kong Basic Law: Blue Print for 'Stability and Prosperity' Under Chinese Sovereignty?* (Hong Kong: Hong Kong University Press, 1991) pp. 38–9.

10   *Selected Works of Deng Xiaoping, Vol. III (1982–1992)* (Beijing: Foreign Languages Press, 1994) pp. 219–20.

11   *Ibid.*, p. 219.

12   Emily Lau, 'A "subversive" alliance: China attacks territory's democrats' *FEER* (3 August 1989) p. 29; and Emily Lau, 'Too close for comfort: Hong Kong's critics hesitate under Peking's threats' *FEER* (24 August 1989) p. 21.

13   Lu Ping (Director of the HKMAO) quoted in *Xinhua* despatch of 13 December 1994 to the effect that 'chaos' threatens if Patten's proposals were to be implemented: BBC *SWB* FE/2177/F2.

14   *Selected Works of Deng Xiaoping, Vol. III (1982–1992)*, see p. 220, n. 108.

15   *Ibid.*, p. 220.

16   Nancy Bernkopf Tucker, *Taiwan, Hong Kong, and the United States, 1945–1992* (NY: Twayne Publishers, 1994) p. 220.

17   Gerald Segal, *The Fate of Hong Kong* (London: Simon & Schuster, 1993) chapters 8 and 9.

18   David J. Clark, 'The Basic Law: one document, two systems' (op. cit.) pp. 41–2.

19   See, for example, the comments to this effect by Wang Fengchao, a deputy director of the HKMAO, cited by Jonathan Karp, 'Man in the middle: Patten edges towards conciliation with Beijing' *FEER* (13 October 1994) p. 16.

20   David S.G. Goodman and Feng Chongyi, in David S.G. Goodman and Gerald Segal (eds) *China Deconstructs: Politics, Trade and Regionalism* (op. cit.) p. 198.

21   See, for example, *Huaren Jingji Nianlu 1994, Yearbook of the Hua Ren Economy 1994* (Beijing: Chinese Social Science Publishing Press, October 1994) especially chapters 3–7.

22   For an argument that, in any case, post-Deng China is heading in that direction rather than towards democracy, see Lucian W. Pye, 'Chinese politics in the late Deng era', Review Essay in *The China Quarterly* (no. 142, June 1995) pp. 573–83.

23   For an account of this aspect of the political succession that the author found persuasive, see Frederick C. Teiwes, 'The paradoxical post-Mao transition: from obeying the leader to "normal politics"' in *The China Journal* (No. 34, July 1995) pp. 55–94. For somewhat different views, see also the articles by Lowell Dittmer, Tang Tsou and Andrew Nathan in the same volume. Since this general issue touches on crucial aspects of Chinese politics, the literature on this is voluminous.

24   Louise do Rosario, 'Look out below: Hong Kong real-estate prices start to soften' in *FEER* (5 May 1994) pp. 73–5.

25 Joseph Cheng, book review in *The China Journal* (No. 34, July 1995) p. 393.

26 See, for example, Louise do Rosario, 'Futures and options: up to a million local Chinese could opt to leave', *FEER* (15 June 1995) p. 21.

27 *Xinhua*, commentary of 18 September 1995 on the elections to the Legislative Council the previous day.

28 Articles 76 and 73 (paragraph 9) of the Basic Law. Moreover, bills relating to government policies can only be introduced with the written consent of the Chief Executive (article 74).

29 Article 17.

30 Interview with the author, Beijing, July 1995.

31 Kevin Rafferty, *City on the Rocks* (op. cit.) pp. 172, 260–2.

32 Interview with former head of the Hong Kong Chamber of Commerce by the author in January 1994.

33 John D. Ho, 'Law and order' in Choi Po-king and Ho Lok-sang (eds) *The Other Hong Kong Report 1993* (op. cit.) p. 68.

34 Rafferty, *City on The Rocks* (op. cit.) pp. 360–1.

35 Mark Roberti, *The Fall of Hong Kong* (op. cit.) pp. 310–12.

36 Louise de Rosario, 'Storm warning: journalist's jail term raises new fears in colony', *FEER* (21 April 1994) p. 21.

37 Mark Clifford and Lincoln Kaye, ' Lai low: Giordano founder ponders his opinions', *FEER* (25 August 1994) pp. 52–3; and Jonathan Karp, 'Forbidden fruit', *FEER* (29 June 1995) pp. 54–8.

38 Louise do Rosario, 'Self control: for some in the media, Beijing's wish is their command', *FEER* (3 March 1994) p. 28. See also Francis Moriarty, 'The media' in Donald H. McMillen and Man Si-wai (eds) *The Other Hong Kong Report 1994* (op. cit) pp. 389–413.

39 Bernard H.K. Luk, 'Hong Kong's international presence' in Donald H. McMillen and Man Si-wai (eds) *The Other Hong Kong Report 1994* (op. cit.) p. 433.

40 The US Consul General, Richard Mueller, spelt this out in some detail in a speech to the Foreign Correspondents' Club in May 1995. *South China Morning Post Weekly Edition* (6 May 1995).

41 Reports by Xinhua News Agency of 22 March 1995 in BBC *SWB* FE/2261/F1.

42 James Casey Sullivan and Robert Sutter, 'Hong Kong's political transition: implications for US interests' *CRS Issue Brief* (Washington, DC: Congressional Research Service) Library of Congress order code IB94051, updated 11 April 1995.

6 CONCLUSION: A TURNING POINT FOR CHINA?

1 As reported by Willy Wo-Lap Lam, 'Economy to remain separate after '97' in *South China Morning Post International Weekly* (September 1995) p. 1.

2 '"Full Text" of Ninth Five Year Plan Proposal' (Beijing: Xinhua News Agency) 4 October 1995 on *SWB* FE/2428 S1/1–16.

3 *Ibid.* p. 1. For evidence of various proposals from within Guangdong to institutionalise the economic integration with Hong Kong, see David

S.G. Goodman and Feng Chongyi, 'Guangdong: Greater Hong Kong and the new regionalist future' in Goodman and Segal (eds) *China Deconstructs* (op. cit.) p. 199.

4   For details of the investment plans of Hong Kong's seven most important business groups in infrastructure and real estate in China, see table in *Investment Risk in Post-Deng China* (Tokyo: Institute of Developing Economies, March 1995) p. 35.

5   David J. Clark, 'The Basic Law: one document, two systems' in Ming K. Chan and David J. Clark (eds) *The Hong Kong Basic Law: Blue Print for 'Stability and Prosperity' Under Chinese Sovereignty?* (op. cit.) p. 40.

6   *Ibid.* p. 40.

POSTSCRIPT

1   *South China Morning Post* (29 December 1995).

2   Lian Yu-ying, 'Preparatory committee established for Hong Kong SAR' *Issues and Studies* (January 1996) p. 123.

3   Cited in Kevin Rafferty, *City on the Rocks* (London: Penguin, revised edn, 1991) p. 492.

Further reading

Cheng, Joseph (ed.) *Hong Kong in Transition* (Hong Kong: Oxford University Press, 1986).

Cottrell, Robert *The End of Hong Kong: the Secret Diplomacy of Imperial Retreat* (London: John Murray, 1993).

Cradock, Percy *Experiences of China* (London: John Murray, 1994).

Domes, Jurgen and Shaw Yu-ming (eds) *Hong Kong: a Chinese and International Concern* (Boulder: Westview Press, 1988).

East Asian Analytical Unit *Overseas Chinese Business Networks* (Canberra: Department of Foreign Affairs and Trade, 1995).

Lau Siu-kai and Kuan Hsin-chi *The Ethos of the Hong Kong Chinese* (Hong Kong: Chinese University Press, 1988).

Miners, Norman J. *The Government and Politics of Hong Kong* (Hong Kong: Oxford University Press, 5th edn., 1994).

Morris, Jan *Hong Kong* (London: Penguin Books, 1985).

The Other Hong Kong Report 1989–1994 (Hong Kong: Chinese University Press, annually since 1989).

Rafferty, Kevin *City on the Rocks: Hong Kong's Uncertain Future* (London: Penguin books, revised and updated, 1991).

Roberti, Mark *The Fall of Hong Kong: China's Triumph and Britain's Betrayal* (New York: John Wiley & Sons, 1994).

Segal, Gerald *The Fate of Hong Kong* (London: Simon & Schuster, 1993).

Shambaugh, David (ed.) *Greater China* (Oxford: Clarendon Press, 1995).

Tsang, Steve Yui-Sang *Democracy Shelved: Great Britain, China and Attempts at Constitutional Reform in Hong Kong, 1945–1952* (Hong Kong: Oxford University Press, 1988).

Tucker, Nancy Bernkopf *Taiwan, Hong Kong and the United States, 1945–1992: Uncertain Friendships* (New York: Twayne Publishers, 1994).

Welsh, Frank *A History of Hong Kong* (London: HarperCollins Publishers, 1993).

Wilson, Dick *China, The Big Tiger* (London and New York: Little Brown, 1996).

——*Hong Kong! Hong Kong!* (London: Unwin Hyman, 1990).

Index